FOR SPEECHES AND SEMINARS BY ROY HERRON

"At a weekend chock full of expert speakers, any talk by Roy Herron is a highlight. He can discuss serious themes expertly, or bring down the house with his sharp wit, or, remarkably, do both in a short period of time. And in both cases, his generous spirit shines through."

—Professor Howard Gardner, MacArthur Prize Winner

"Roy is a fantastic speaker. He regaled us with stories both showing humor and having a poignant message. He drew the audience into his every word, built up suspense, and ended with a great crescendo that brought down the house."

—Michael Breyer, entrepreneur

"Roy Herron has an uncanny ability to connect with almost any audience, where you find yourself both entertained and moved. I have seen him amidst many national leaders and even there he clearly stands out."

—Michael G. Maudlin, editorial director, Harper San Francisco

"Roy Herron combines the clarity of a good teacher, the appeal of a popular politician, the spirit of a committed preacher, and the wit of a down-home humorist. Listening to him is both fun and fruitful."

—William Phillips, Nobel Laureate in Physics

"Roy Herron is one of the most alive, entertaining speakers it has been my privilege to hear. He captivates his audience from the start and informs, challenges, and amuses . . . an awesome task few can master."

—The Reverend Helen M. Moore, St. Paul's Episcopal Church

"Roy's speaking is like an embracing arm around the shoulders. With candor, humor, and insight, Roy weaves a tale that leaves the listener surprised, wiser, and more hopeful."

—Rabbi Elie Spitz, Congregation B'nai Israel

"Roy Herron is a deeply thoughtful and provocative speaker. He can motivate a room like no one else, with personal warmth and sparkling humor. He is a treasure with much to offer."

—Marion Kahn, Marion Kahn Communications

Have Roy speak to or lead seminars for your company, church, conference, or organization.

FOR MORE INFORMATION,
VISIT WWW.ROYHERRONSPEAKS.COM
OR WWW.ROYHERRON.COM.

Faith in Politics

All of the author's royalties will go to college scholarships awarded by the nonprofit *Volunteer Center for Rural Development*.

OTHER BOOKS BY ROY HERRON

Things Held Dear: Soul Stories for My Sons

Tennessee Political Humor: Some of These Jokes You Voted For
(with L. H. "Cotton" Ivy)

God and Politics: How Can a Christian Be in Politics?

FOR MORE INFORMATION,
VISIT WWW.ROYHERRONSPEAKS.COM.

FAITH IN POLITICS

*Southern Political Battles
Past and Present*

ROY HERRON

With a Foreword by David Waters

The University of Tennessee Press
Knoxville

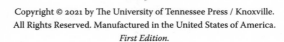

LIBRARY OF CONGRESS CATALOGING-IN-PUBLICATION DATA
Names: Herron, Roy, author.
Title: Faith in politics : Southern political battles past and present / Roy Herron.
Other titles: Southern political battles past and present
Description: First edition. | Knoxville : The University of Tennessee Press, [2021] |
Includes bibliographical references and index. |
Summary: "This is a collection of former Tennessee state senator Roy Herron's
writings and speeches on various topics, including civil liberties, economic justice,
health care, politics, faith, and many things in between. While the essays are reprinted
much as they originally appeared, Herron has added some thoughtful reflections
on themes that constantly recur in our politics and in his various writings, as well
as carefully identifying figures who might be unfamiliar to contemporary readers
and updating some circumstances. In general, Herron's work reveals that political
issues are often very similar over time, but it also bears witness to stark changes in
our representatives' response to social problems and the growing divide between
Republicans and Democrats throughout the nation"—Provided by publisher.
Identifiers: LCCN 2020040734 (print) | LCCN 2020040735 (ebook) |
ISBN 9781621905943 (paperback) | ISBN 9781621905950 (kindle edition) |
ISBN 9781621905967 (pdf)
Subjects: LCSH: Herron, Roy—Political and social views. | Tennessee—
Politics and government—1951- | Southern States—Politics and government—1951- |
Legislators—Tennessee. | Tennessee. General Assembly. Senate. |
Christianity and politics—Southern States.
Classification: LCC F440.22.H47 A25 2020 (print) | LCC F440.22.H47 (ebook) |
DDC 328.73/092—dc23
LC record available at https://lccn.loc.gov/2020040734
LC ebook record available at https://lccn.loc.gov/2020040735

*For our sons, John, Rick, and Ben Miller Herron,
and our niece and nephew, Erin and Sean Dugan,
who inspired and co-authored much of this book,
and for all young Tennesseans,
who are inspiring and co-authoring Tennessee's future.*

CONTENTS

Foreword   xiii
  David Waters
Acknowledgments   xvii

INTRODUCTION   1
  Same Issues   1
  Ideology   3
  Partisanship   5
  Religion and Politics   8
  A Negative View of Politics   9
  A Positive View of Politics   10
  The Best at the Time   11

PART 1. LIBERTY

1. AMERICAN CONSTITUTIONAL FREEDOMS   15
  Remembering What Is Right with America   16
  Christians In Eastern Europe   19
  Japan's War Sentiments Understandable   21
  An Open Letter to Senator Baker and Senator Sasser   24

2. RELIGIOUS LIBERTY   29
  Protecting Students' Religious Liberty   29
  Teach Students about Bible So They Can
    Better Understand World   32

PART 2. LIFE

3. PUBLIC SAFETY   39
  Liquor Bill Puts Lives in Governor's Hands   39
  Safe Babies or Highway Carnage   44
  Helmets off Riders, Brains on Pavement   46

Cables or Crosses: Interstate Safety Barriers   48
Boost Federal Inspections before Worse Incidents Happen   51

4. PUBLIC HEALTH   **53**
Big Tobacco Is Selling Misleading Myths   53
Front Lines of the Smoking War   55
Why Does the GOP Hate Health Care Plan?   58
Why Is "Big Government" Firing Our Small-Town Doc?   61

5. HEALTH CARE FOR WORKERS: TENNCARE   **65**
Slashing TennCare Is Not the Answer   65
Question: Can TennCare Be Saved in Its Current Form? Yes   68

6. HEALTH CARE FOR WORKERS: MEDICAID EXPANSION   **71**
Working People Need State to Accept Federal Funds,
    Expand Medicaid   71
Expanding Medicaid Is to Choose Life   73
Republicans' Stand on Medicaid Will Be
    Disastrous for Local Hospitals   75
Why Tennessee Should Expand Medicaid   77

PART 3. RIGHTS

7. VOTERS' RIGHTS   **83**
Tennessee Needs Paper Trail for Every Vote   83
Voter ID Law Will Disenfranchise Rural Residents   85
It's 50 Years since Civil Rights Act of '64   90

8. WOMEN'S RIGHTS   **93**
A Woman's Right to Save Her Life   94
Amendment One Leaves No Exceptions for Victims of Rape   96
Amendment One Would Destroy, Not "Neutralize" Rights   98

9. CRIME VICTIMS' RIGHTS   **101**
Crime Victims Deserve the Right to Be Heard   101
Balancing the Scales of Justice   104

PART 4. EDUCATION

10. EDUCATION   111
Where Education Is a Priority and Where It Is Not   113
Education Savings Accounts Are Just Another
    Voucher Scheme Ripe for Abuse   116
The Tennessee Education Savings Account Bill Fails the Math Test   118

PART 5. JUSTICE

11. ECONOMIC JUSTICE   123
Raise Minimum Wage and Fight "Income Inequality"   123
What We All Lose in Rural West Tennessee's Decline   125

12. PREDATORY LENDING   131
Credit Card Shower No Blessing   132
Resist Lobbyists and Crack Down on Predatory Lending   134
"Title Pledge Lending" Must Be Changed   136

PART 6. LEADERSHIP

13. OUR LEADING LEADERS   141
A "Tennessee Treasure"   142
Book Review of *Howard Baker: Conciliator in an Age of Crisis*   145

14. CHRISTIAN DEMOCRATS   149
Strong Faith Led to Democratic Party   149
Why I Am a Democrat   151
Attack of Obama Visit Typical for Today's GOP   157

15. ON LEGISLATING   159
Diary of a Legislator: A Freshman Lawmaker's
    Personal Account of Encountering the Political Process   159
Tips on the Care and Feeding of Legislators   169

Conclusion   173
Index   177
About the Author   187

FOREWORD

I met Roy Herron when I was a rookie newspaper reporter and he was a greenhorn lawyer. Both of us were trying to find our vocations in the court squares, church circles, fields, and factories of West Tennessee in the early 1980s. But I believe our friendship was cemented about a decade later when I borrowed a used pickup truck from him.

My car had broken down. I couldn't afford to fix it anytime soon, and I still had two years left to pay it off. I had kids to take to school, work that required reliable transportation, and graduate classes I couldn't miss. My friend Roy offered to let me borrow an old one-ton, two-tone Chevy pickup that was just sitting in his mother's driveway collecting pecan leaves. I'd always wanted to drive an old truck, even a boxy tan-and-white model like Roy's, so I was thrilled. I used the truck for a few months and returned it without any new dents.

That's when Roy mentioned that what I'd been driving around the perilous streets of Memphis, what he had kindly entrusted to me without telling me, wasn't just an old truck but a family heirloom. It was the truck Roy's father, Grooms Herron, a chancery court judge, bought new in 1976 so that year he and Roy's mother, Mary Cornelia Brasfield Herron, could drive across America all the way to Alaska, a trip they had long dreamed about. It also was the truck his father drove for the last time the next spring one Sunday morning to check on the family's farm. While Judge Herron was feeding their cattle, he suffered a heart attack and died.

Roy Brasfield Herron is a kind and generous human being. He'd give his worst critic the shirt off his back if it was needed, even if the scoundrel had just cast a vote against Roy. Some people think Roy's kindness, generosity, and general good nature might be calculated products of his long and notable career in politics and his desire to get even scoundrels to vote for him. But those of us who knew Roy before he first ran for public office, who knew his devoted and generous mother, Mary Cornelia, who know his wise and accomplished wife, Nancy Carol, those of us whose Tennessee roots run as deep and strong as Roy's, know better. We know that politics sorely tested but failed to compromise Roy's true character and genuine qualities.

Not that politics hasn't pushed and pulled Roy to make difficult choices. During his more than quarter century as a state representative and state senator, Roy sometimes struggled over "voting on the basis not of conscience but of campaigning," as he put it after a hard vote in 1988 in his first term in the Tennessee House of Representatives. As he explains in an essay you'll find in this book, Roy immediately regretted that vote. I suspect he would like to have several "do-overs" among his literally thousands of votes.

But most of this book is about issues where Roy does not agonize but, instead, feels strongly and acts clearly. It is a collection of opinion pieces Roy wrote over the past four decades. The book explores the public policy views and political considerations of a longtime state legislator and party leader in a place and time of rising religious, political, and social polarization.

Yet these essays are more than a series of op-eds. They are dispatches from a man who lived in his small town and worked in his capital city, a Christian Southerner and Democrat who came of age during the Carter years, was first elected to the Tennessee House during the Reagan-Bush years, moved to the Senate during the Clinton and Gore years, came to greatest power in the second Bush years, and, after winning nineteen elections, was finally defeated running for Congress during the Obama years.

Many essays read more like homilies, and why not? This is a man who went to divinity school as well as law school, a believer in the Bible and the Constitution, and a man of faith and reason who reveres life (even *after* babies are born) and passionately preaches for his beloved state to save lives through safety laws and health care and to enhance lives through better education and good jobs.

Some would call him "conservative" for his essays advocating for our constitutional freedoms, crime victims' rights, and students' religious liberties. Others would label as "liberal" essays pushing for women's rights, protections for the poor from predatory lenders, and raising the minimum wage.

In fact, these essays are laments from a man who sees himself as a common-sense centrist in a state that, until recently, had a long and proud tradition of sending moderate politicians to Nashville and Washington—governors, senators, and legislators from both parties and all three Grand Divisions of Tennessee who listened to all sides and represented the sensible center of a state that was the last to secede and the first to rejoin the Union.

These essays reflect the deep public and private concerns of a loving son and brother, a devoted husband and father, and a seventh-generation product of rural Tennessee as he endeavors to keep his faith in politics and to keep faith with the people who elected him.

People like the Herrons and the Brasfields who settled and worked the farm-lands and floodplains that lie between the forested hills along the Tennessee River and the flat Delta along the Mississippi River.

People who express their faith in God and country and each other in different ways for different reasons at different times.

People who know the practical value of an old pickup truck and the priceless value of traditions and legacies passed proudly, if not easily, from one generation to the next.

DAVID WATERS
Journalist in Residence
Institute for Public Service Reporting
University of Memphis

ACKNOWLEDGMENTS

In 2005, Tennessee's distinguished Senator Howard Baker convened a symposium called "Votes and Jokes: Laughter and America's Political Personality." Because Cotton Ivy and I had recently written *Tennessee Political Humor* for the University of Tennessee Press, this lowly state senator was invited to participate alongside national figures. One was award-winning editorial cartoonist Charlie Daniel, and Charlie has been a dear friend ever since. Of course, after six decades as an outstanding editorial cartoonist—Charlie was a cartoonist both at the *Knoxville Journal* (1958–1992) and also the *Knoxville News Sentinel* (1992–2019)—he is a dear friend to many. In these pages are nineteen of his cartoons. Here you will see that one Charlie Daniel cartoon is worth far more than a thousand of my words.

Bruce Plante went to the *Chattanooga Times* a couple of years before I went to the legislature, and our tenures overlapped for two decades. I thank him for his cartoons shown here—but he should thank me for providing him with cartoon fodder. In this book is my favorite Bruce Plante cartoon, giving insight into and poking fun at the Student Religious Liberty Act, a law that I wrote!

Nancy, my bride for a third of a century, and our sons, John, Rick, and Ben, all should be listed as co-authors. They helped write these opinion essays by inspiring, encouraging, and enduring me. John and Rick even helped draft and edit many of them. Rick also worked hard to turn the manuscript into a book. I cannot thank all four enough, and I love them with all my heart.

My mother and father, Mary Brasfield Herron and Chancellor Grooms Herron, loved and led by never forgetting the call to serve both God and neighbor. My sister, Betsye, and my brothers, Ben and Dean, always were there for me in campaigns, public service, and other dubious undertakings. In fact, Ben is still there for me and who else but that ultra-runner/ultra-brother would run with me at 4:00 a.m.? Nancy's parents, Fran and L. J. Miller, and my sister and brother-in-law, Jan and Dennis Dugan, have been family in every way that matters. I thank them for their counsel, tolerance, and love. Ancestors who showed the way of public service included Senator Dean Grooms, Squire Clarence B. Herron, and "Miss Johnnie" Brasfield.

Josephine Binkley is like a sister to Nancy and me, and Martha Stutts is like a daughter. "J.B." ran our legislative office for a quarter-century. Thousands did not have to waste their time with the middle man—calling Josephine was the way to get government to do right or quit doing wrong. I cannot say enough about the incredible work she did. Nor can I thank her enough for grandmothering our three sons, her "little fellers."

Martha Stutts ran our campaign offices and still runs our law office. I call her "Summa" not only because she graduated from UT-Martin *summa cum laude*, but also because she simply is The Best. Martha's incredible professional competence, half-marathons in all 50 states, and faithful witness are amazing. It would be a "howlin' wilderness" without her.

More recently, Angie Lassiter has brought her joyful spirit to our office and to all her good works, for which I give much thanks.

Jake Dunavant, Rob James, and Michael Lamb became like older brothers to our sons and like older sons to Nancy and me. They talked through, edited, and helped shape many of these essays. Their voices can be heard here, especially as they helped compose and improve speeches that eventually evolved into op-eds. Their talent and work ethic are unmatched.

Zander Alley found and organized these essays. My fellow Dresden native and Vanderbilt alum served as research assistant, editor, brain trust, and friend. Without our family—without Josephine, Martha, and Angie, without Jake, Rob, Michael, and Zander—this book would not be.

Clearly all these essays were co-authored. But I especially thank the co-authors whose names lent credibility to mine: Representative Craig Fitzhugh, Representative Jere Hargrove, Rick Herron, Mayor Jill Holland, Garrett Jennings, Representative Mark Maddox, Hannah Oakley, Annie Prescott, Rachel Rodriguez, and Senator Page Walley.

Even with these outstanding co-authors, the op-eds only appeared thanks to the leadership of these editorial page editors: the *Commercial Appeal's* David Vincent, David Kushma, Otis Sanford, Jerome Wright, and David Waters; the *Chattanooga Times Free Press's* Harry Austin and Pam Sohn, the *Knoxville News Sentinel's* Scott Barker, the *Jackson Sun's* Tom Bohs, and the *Tennessean's* Sandra Roberts, John Gibson, Ted Rayburn, David Plazas, and its legendary publisher John Seigenthaler.

I owe so much to so many Tennesseans, but especially to the citizens of the Seventy-Sixth House District and the Twenty-Fourth Senatorial District. These constituents were incredibly faithful and patient teachers. Their struggles and solutions inspired and informed my views on these issues.

Across four decades, members of the Tennessee General Assembly have been teachers and mentors, colleagues and friends, fellow servants and prayer partners. I have been blessed by and am grateful for their fellowship and faithfulness.

A special debt is owed Representatives Mark Maddox and Craig Fitzhugh, who co-founded the Volunteer Center for Rural Development to continue Governor McWherter's important work of helping young people and training leaders.

My indebtedness and gratitude extend to many other public servants. I was especially privileged to work for and be mentored by Congressman Ed Jones, Governor Ned McWherter, and Vice President Al Gore. Their leadership and integrity greatly influenced these pages and my own attempts to serve. I am deeply grateful to each.

Johnny Hayes was a Tennessee Commissioner of Economic and Community Development and a Director of the Tennessee Valley Authority. He led the way when Al Gore ran for Congress, the U.S. Senate, Vice President, and President. Joe Hill was the District Director for the Eighth Congressional District and served longer than any other congressional district director in Tennessee history. Johnny, Joe, and I shared the values of our Methodist Church and the challenges of many a campaign. They were awesome teachers, and occasionally Nancy and I would be their families' preachers. Johnny and Joe became friends, then family. I could never thank them enough.

Many ministers and church leaders have nurtured my faith and shaped this book. They also helped me wrestle with religious vocation in the political world. The legislative prayer group that Speaker Pro Tem Lois DeBerry started and that continues today has been a blessing since 1987. I also owe special debts to the Reverends Joe Beale, Frank Bulle, Ken Carder, Fred Craddock, Harold Conner, Gene Davenport, Dan Donaldson, Kaki Friskics-Warren, Adam Hall, Jerry Harber, Jerry Hassell, Jim Laney, and Greg Waldrop.

Scholars particularly influential in shaping this book and this writer include Larry McGehee, Ted Mosch, and Phil Watkins of the University of Tennessee at Martin, Matthew Black of the University of St. Andrews, and Vanderbilt University's Don Beisswenger, Bob Belton, John Donahue, Don Hall, Walter Harrelson, Tom Ogletree, Kelly Miller Smith, Peggy Way, and Susan Ford Wiltshire.

For two decades, I learned from students I taught at Vanderbilt University. I especially thank the Legislation Seminar classes at the Law School and the Divinity School classes Justice Ministry and Advocacy, Religion and Law, and Religion and Politics.

Authors Will Campbell and John Egerton taught me to write, to trust God more than government, and as Will put it, "to minister without regard for race, creed, color or Klan affiliation." Will Campbell also officiated at our wedding, perhaps a questionable kindness to Nancy, but one she overlooks since he baptized our boys. John Egerton used barrels of red ink on my weak and wordy prose to make it less anemic. I'm a less terrible writer because John insisted I cut, cut, cut and re-re-re-rewrite.

Emmett Edwards talked through every important decision and influenced my every course of action from the time we were teenagers. Stephanie Egnotovich edited my first book. Without them, that book and this book would not be. Even after their passing, my debt to them grows.

The University of Tennessee Press in general, and Director Scot Danforth and Jon Boggs in particular, have been extraordinarily gracious, professional, and helpful. I know how much better a book this is because of their work, and you should, too.

I am also most grateful to Maggie Crowell for her diligent and extremely competent proofreading. She corrected an embarrassingly large number of my errors, and the errors that remain are entirely mine.

I met so many more fantastic folks while in and often through politics. Space constraints forbid me from mentioning all the wonderful people, so let me thank some of you in groups. One benefit of being thanked in a group is that others may not be able to pick you out and judge you for associating with ne'er-do-wells like me. So, here's to the Baker Republicans. Blue Dogs. Bohunkers. Capitol Hill Press Corps. Charleston Crowd. Coon Supper Crew. E.W. James Bunch. Gore Corps. Has-Beens. Home Folks. Interns. Ironmen. Just Judges. Law-Divinity Students. McWherter Scholars. Methodists. Public School Advocates. Real Baptists. Reelfoot Lake Duck Hunters. Recovering Vols. Republican Friends. Rural West Tennessee Caucus. Teammates. Third House. Todd's Sunday School Class. Trial Lawyers. Volker's Time Trialers. Yellow Dawgs. And last, but not least, the Radical Fundamentalist Progressive Evangelical Brotherhood and Sisterhood (Conservative, Unorthodox, and Unreformed). Here's to each of you—and all other loved ones!

INTRODUCTION

The thing that hath been,
it is that which shall be;
and that which is done is that which shall be done:
and there is no new thing under the sun.

—*King James Version (KJV)*[1]

SAME ISSUES

Not long after I was first elected, a veteran legislator told this rookie representative, "You know, Roy, there aren't any new issues. There are the same issues. Sometimes different bills with little differences, little refinements. But the same issues."

Eventually I decided the veteran legislator was right. When you read the following opinion essays from the last four decades, you will see most are about issues still debated today. I considered these issues extremely important when I legislated, and they are still terribly important today:

Constitutional freedoms and religious liberties
Voting rights and civil rights
Education
Economic justice and predatory lending
Public safety and public health

---

1   What has been will be again, what has been done will be done again; there is nothing new under the sun. Ecclesiastes 1:9 New International Version (NIV)

Health care, TennCare, and Medicaid expansion
Women's rights and crime victims' rights

The fundamental issues long have been about how we protect our freedoms and the vulnerable, help our neighbors and nation, and build our children's and grandchildren's future. The legislation may change, but the fundamental issues change little, and the fundamental values change not at all. In the words of Ecclesiastes, "There is nothing new under the sun."

A friend who knew I had compiled these essays from decades of public life asked, "Have your views on the issues changed?" I quipped, "I guess I haven't learned much over four decades."

Critics and foes doubtless believe that is true, and it may be true enough. But the main reason my views on these issues have not changed much is this: I did not go to the trouble of writing an op-ed essay unless I was especially passionate about the issue. And if I was that passionate about the issue, I felt compelled to

The author celebrates with a victory fist-pump as he was first elected to the Tennessee House of Representatives in 1986. Photo: *Weakley County Press*.

research hard, dig deep, and think long. By the time I was through researching and writing, my feelings had grown still deeper—or instead of the draft going to the newspaper, it went in the round file or a shredder.

So even if I wrote in the 1980s, 1990s, 2000s, or 2010s, these essays can be relevant to new legislation and policies. I hope you might find them useful for research, studies, stories, facts, examples, and any time there is a need for materials about issues from the 1980s to the present when the same issues come up in the future.

These essays have not been changed significantly either. I have corrected a few typos and tightened a few sentences. But these essays, for good or for bad, are essentially the way they were printed back in the days when newspapers were still paper. As our son John points out, in the age of tweets and Facebook posts, when *280 characters* is the norm, we need to recall when *600 to 800 words* were the coin of the persuasive realm.

These writings are creatures of their times, but after some I describe circumstances that have changed since these works were composed. In the notes after the essays, I also identify characters and events that might not be familiar to some contemporary readers.

I also add this additional information to make clear that most of the issues that demanded my attention then still demand our attention and work today. I hope and even pray that you will be at least as passionate about these important issues that still are crucial for our neighbors and for our children's future.

IDEOLOGY

I grew up in West Tennessee in the county seat town of Dresden, down the street from the Speaker of the Tennessee House of Representatives, Ned R. McWherter. When Speaker McWherter decided to run for Governor, I decided to run for his seat in the House of Representatives. Carroll and Weakley Counties kindly elected me to serve as their representative.

Not long after I got to the legislature, a new friend quietly told me, "You've got folks up here confused."

"How so?" I asked.

He shook his head and replied, "They say that every time they look up, Herron's voting with the Blacks and the Republicans."

Which, if you think about it, is quite a trick. But I suppose what folks really were saying was that I didn't fit into some of the stereotypes, and I didn't just go along with one group all the time. Which I hope was true.

A witticism attributed, probably wrongly, to Winston Churchill goes like this: "If you're not a liberal in your twenties, you have no heart. If you're not a conservative in your forties, you have no head."

I am conservative about many things. But I hope as my head has learned, my heart has not dulled. I hope I learned both from Governor McWherter's conservatism and his conscience.

I am fiscally conservative. I did not grow up in the Great Depression, but my parents and grandparents made me think I did. I grew up hearing how my grandparents almost lost their farm. And like so many neighbors, they would have lost the farm, except my father from his small but steady salary paid their taxes—until the New Deal came down, and crop prices went up.

I heard how my parents could not afford to burn coal at night, so on cold winter mornings they would find the water in their bedroom's wash basin frozen solid. Times were hard, so hard that my family became known for being especially fiscally conservative. Some would say downright "tight." Because even when times were better, my grandparents and parents never forgot those hard times.

My paternal grandmother wore things until they plumb wore out, saved all the glass jars and returned all the drink bottles, carefully watched the few coins in her change purse, and dressed like the working woman she was. Even in her seventies, she got out in the fields with me. In the summer sun she tugged the heavy logging chain and hooked it around the saplings and small trees so the tractor could pull them out and we could return the fields to cultivation.

Having suffered through the Depression, my parents and grandparents had compassion for less fortunate neighbors. The Memphis newspaper's obituary quoted neighbors saying my maternal grandmother was "An Angel of Mercy." She died before I was born, but those neighbors, several of them her Sunday School students over four decades, told me stories about her.

Not long ago a new client told an old story of how my paternal grandfather helped save his grandfather from being tortured or lynched by a mob. And my new client's cousin, another successful African American businessman, still tears up telling what my grandfather did to help him when he was a poor boy.

After my grandparents passed and even after my parents passed, neighbors and strangers alike would tell about things that my grandparents and parents had done for them or for their families.

Night after night, dinner after dinner, my father would say, "Mighty fine meal, Mrs. Herron." And either Dad would add, or Mom would say, "Don't we wish everybody had it so good?" But they did more than just "wish."

My family and my mentors practiced what I called "compassionate conservatism," at least until a presidential candidate tainted that expression for some of us.

One reader called this collection "confusing," because the views are not just "conservative" or "liberal" and don't just fit partisan stereotypes.

Today our national politics is, at best, polarized. The Democrats can't be too liberal. The Republicans can't be too reactionary. The worst thing that can be said about a Republican or Democrat today is to call her or him a "moderate."

But when I grew of age politically, Governor Ned McWherter and Senator Howard Baker were Tennessee's gold standard. Both were known for—and both were attacked and praised for—working with people of good faith in *both* political parties. Republican senator Baker and Democratic governor McWherter were less concerned about right and left than right and wrong.

I hope the following essays reveal that their great leadership and good examples were not totally wasted on me. And I hope that people of conservatism and conscience will lead our great state to even greater days for all our children.

PARTISANSHIP

One manuscript reader thought, "Perhaps some revisions should be made to the passages that are highly critical of Republicans." But another wrote, "There is abundant evidence of [Herron's] independence from strict party dogma."

Still, I thought about omitting the essays that mention political parties, but that would have purged the record and made the collection less historically accurate.

I thought about editing the essays to omit party references. But that would have diminished the accuracy of what was fought and thought at the time. And the truth is that sometimes there were differences between the parties. So I left the essays as published and sometimes explain why I wrote them the way that I did.

When I was in the General Assembly, I tried very hard to make my arguments as non-partisan or bi-partisan as I could. For example, in a single speech defending teachers from Republican attacks, I cited President Ronald Reagan as an example and quoted President Reagan not once but twice. Most essays written before I left the legislature in 2013 reflect that bipartisanship.

After I left the General Assembly, I tried with some essays to encourage Governor Haslam to do as then-Governor Mike Pence and most Republican governors did and accept federal funds to help the working poor purchase

6 INTRODUCTION

health care. Eventually Governor Haslam did push for accepting those federal funds. But many Republicans in the General Assembly remained afraid that voting for acceptance of 100 percent federal funding would let primary foes beat them by attacking them for voting for "Obamacare." These essays pushing for health care for working people refer to party simply because the General Assembly divided in such a partisan way.

I also responded explicitly to partisan attempts to discourage and disable voting. I wrote plainly about the partisanship being demonstrated by those who would deny the most basic of our freedoms. I thought then, and I think now, that this is a fundamental difference between some (but not all!) Republicans and myself.

After Vice President George H.W. Bush swore into office the newly elected United States Senators, the future president kindly posed for photographs with the new senators of both parties. Here, Vice President Bush and Senator Gore are joined by Senator Gore's wife, Tipper, and their three daughters, Karenna, Kristen, and Sarah, and the author. Photo: Lena Harris, *Associated Press.*

At a McDonald's reception for legislators in 1987,
Republican state representative (now senator) Art
Swann seems a bit underwhelmed about joining Ronald
McDonald and the author for a bipartisan handshake.
Representative Swann is on the right, and the author is
not the one in the middle. Photo property of author.

I don't like being partisan. When, immediately after serving in the General
Assembly, I was asked to run for state Democratic Party Chair, I did so because
I thought our state had gone off the road into an extreme-right ditch. As I told
many a Democratic gathering, we need to elect some more Democrats or some
more of the Reasonable Republicans. Not every Democrat liked me saying that,
but it was honest. I became party chair not to be partisan, but because I thought
Commissioner Lewie Donelson, a Republican respected by members of both
parties, was right when he said it was good for the people to have a choice and
good for the state to have two strong parties working together.

So often now there is no choice except in primaries. The two parties rarely
work together in Washington or Nashville. So, I'd rather not be partisan.
And I acknowledge that many Republicans also believe in health care for the

working poor and voting rights for all. Saying this now seems better than trying
to purge the record by redacting these essays.

RELIGION AND POLITICS

Some will read these and find too much religious talk here. To those critics, I
must point out that even the founders drew on religious ideals as they created
our republic.[2]

In 1775, John Adams wrote his wife, Abigail, "Statesmen may plan and specu-
late for Liberty, but it is Religion and Morality alone which can establish the
principles upon which Freedom can securely stand." Adams believed that "a
patriot must be a religious man [or woman]."

The original draft of the Declaration of Independence referred to the "laws
of nature and of nature's god" and the "Creator" who endows us with "certain
inalienable rights." The Second Continental Congress kept those and also in-
serted into Thomas Jefferson's document two more references to God, appealing "to the supreme judge of the world" and referring to the delegates' "firm
reliance on the protection of divine providence."

When the Constitutional Convention struggled in a fierce debate in 1787,
Benjamin Franklin emphasized the importance of religion for America's future:
"I have lived, Sir, a long time, and the longer I live, the more convincing proofs
I see of this truth—that God governs in the affairs of men. And if a sparrow
cannot fall to the ground without His notice, is it probable that an empire can
rise without His aid? We have been assured, Sir, in the Sacred Writings, that
'except the Lord build the House, they labor in vain that build it.' I firmly believe
this; and I also believe that without His concurring aid we shall succeed in this
political building no better than the Builders of Babel."

When our nation's first president gave his farewell address, George Washington
warned, "Of all the dispositions and habits, which lead to political prosperity,
Religion and morality are indispensable supports. . . . Reason and experience
both forbid us to expect that national morality can prevail in exclusion of a
religious principle."

I grew up in a home where asking a blessing before meals and saying prayers
before bed were daily facts of life. A caring, loving church family nurtured me.

---

2   Portions of this section were first published in my *How Can a Christian Be in Politics?*
(Carol Stream, IL: Tyndale House, 2005).

In college I learned from and worshipped with fired-up friends at a Baptist student union, excited evangelicals in an interdenominational group, and faithful Methodists and Roman Catholics at an interfaith center. I studied New Testament and ethics in Scotland before returning to the States for a joint program in divinity and law. I worked in campus ministry, preached at local churches, and served in small ways from the rural South to New York's Hell's Kitchen.

Then I returned to my hometown where I practiced law to support my preaching habit. As our church's full-time minister observed of this part-time preacher, "We pay Roy a dollar a year, and it only takes three sermons to get our money's worth."

Finally I fell from the pulpit to the pit of politics. In defense, I offer two mitigating circumstances: a rough family and a tough neighborhood.

My family included county legislators, sheriffs, a state legislator, a judge, and a federal law enforcement agent. Within two blocks of our home during my mother's lifetime resided five mayors, five legislators, four or five judges, a public service commissioner, and the Speaker of the state House of Representatives who later became governor. Frequently visiting relatives on our block were two US senators, including one who became vice president.

Such family members and neighbors bore witness that public service could be an honest, even honorable, way to love your neighbor as yourself.

Government can be awful, or it can be good; often it is some of both.

A NEGATIVE VIEW OF POLITICS

Many of us feel we have all the government we can stand and more than we can afford. We strongly, instinctively react against politics when we consider waste, fraud, corruption, deception, arrogance, misuse of authority, and burdensome taxes. Many people of faith hold this view of politics and government, and they also believe that government in recent decades has contributed to moral decline and the weakening of traditional values.

Anger and frustration toward government today are very high. But if you find yourself frustrated with government, imagine how frustrated elected officials feel when we try to make government work and often cannot. Time and again, my task was not, as I would wish, to pass needed laws or set up helpful programs but rather to try to stop bad bills and simply make existing laws and programs work. Often I worked to get government to help people, but perhaps even more often I tried to keep it from hindering or even harming citizens.

Like my father before me, I get edgy around April 15 when my wife and I

In 1996, *Chattanooga Times* cartoonist Bruce Plante captured the
effects of two Democratic senators joining Governor Don Sundquist's
Republican Party, giving Republicans the majority in the state senate.
Illustration by Bruce Plante, *Chattanooga Times*.

calculate our federal taxes. I've seen governments waste money much too often.
I've even known corrupt people in government who stole public funds. I know
too well how fallen our government and its officials can be.

A POSITIVE VIEW OF POLITICS

As frustrating and maddening as government and politics can be, they are
necessary, and they are often forces for good.

I served in the Tennessee General Assembly with a wonderful senator named
Anna Belle Clement O'Brien. Senator O'Brien started hundreds of talks and
speeches with these words: "Politics is a beautiful word to me!" She would explain, "Politics is how crippled children walk, the mentally ill get care, roads
are built, health care is provided, children are taught."

It is through the political process, through electing people to represent us,
that government works, doing the things we ourselves—as the *polis*—ask it
to do. Among other things, we ask governments to provide for the national

In 1997, with the author's election to a seat previously held by Democrat-turned-Republican Milton Hamilton, Democrats regained a majority in the state senate. Bruce Plante portrayed the change by putting Republican governor Don Sundquist in the backseat. Illustration by Bruce Plante, *Chattanooga Times*

defense; build roads, airports, courthouses, and jails; foster a business climate for economic prosperity; protect workers; support needy children; protect us from hazardous wastes and deadly poisons; educate our children; prevent and punish crime; promote good health and prevent epidemics; and defend our constitutional rights to free speech, association, and worship.

Indeed, whether we respect our governments or not, we ask them to play important and positive roles in the lives of every American citizen. I submit that, for all the flaws, our American political system is a blessing that too often we take for granted. And no one owes our government more than I do. It saved my father when he was horribly wounded in World War II. It saved our babies when their lives were almost lost.

THE BEST AT THE TIME

One more story, then you can turn to the essays. When I was in the Senate, my Republican colleague and future Speaker Ron Ramsey stood one day to tell the Chamber what had happened to him and other colleagues the night before.

Reports on nocturnal activities, usually given discreetly and without the aid of microphones, were always of interest. But such a report on the floor in front of reporters and the whole world, of course, immediately got everyone's attention.

The evening before, as was their custom, Senator Ramsey and two or three others had gone to a movie. When they came outside after the show, Ron's car was gone. It had been stolen.

Senator Ramsey reassured us, however, that the police had found his car. Unfortunately, everything in it was missing. Except one thing, he said. A book called *Tennessee Political Humor* that Cotton Ivy and I had written was the only thing left behind.

This drew a great deal of laughter from everyone, myself included. Still, after some humorous commentary about how my book was so worthless even thieves wouldn't steal it, I felt I had to respond.

"Mr. Speaker," I protested, "I want this distinguished body to know that I write for a higher class of criminals than common car thieves."

It was the best I could come up with at the time.

Similarly, these were the best essays I could come up with at the time. You might write better essays now—and I hope you will. I wrote then and I share now for those who don't mind reading, who want to think, who don't mind being challenged by new information, and who don't have to make up their own facts. I wrote for those who want to make Tennessee even better for all of our sisters and brothers.

I wrote these essays for you.

PART 1. LIBERTY

1

AMERICAN CONSTITUTIONAL FREEDOMS

In 1976, I traveled behind the Iron Curtain. There the wisdom of Joni Mitchell—and our Founders—became painfully clear. As Mitchell sang, "Don't it always seem to go / that you don't know what you've got till it's gone?" In Eastern Europe, our constitutional rights were "gone." The painful oppression of the East Germans, Poles, Czechs, and Slovaks was seared into me. I realized more than ever before what I've got in our American constitutional rights.

The first two of the following essays came out of that summer's travels with no hope of Eastern Europeans ever having constitutional rights under Soviet oppression behind the Iron Curtain.

The third essay was written in Japan when that country's postwar issues reminded me of our Southern struggles.

This chapter's final essay deals with legal representation, sometimes granted by our Constitution and sometimes not—but even when not granted, often needed.

REMEMBERING WHAT IS RIGHT WITH AMERICA (1986)

Some people continue to harp about all that's wrong with America. I'm one of them. The reign of God has not been fully realized on Earth, not even in our country. Too many suffer too much for us to nurture the illusion that "all is right with America."

But, thank goodness, there are a lot of things right with our country. Perhaps the easiest way to see that is to look elsewhere.

My brother, a friend, and I traveled to Eastern Europe to see what life was like behind the Iron Curtain. In Czechoslovakia we met a university student whose English probably was better than our own. We enjoyed light conversation walking about his campus, but when we stopped and sat, I asked: "Was it better before 1968, or is it better now?"

Though he'd had little trouble with my Tennessee twang until then, he didn't seem to understand. I posed the question again in more detail: "Was it better before 1968 when the Russians with their troops and tanks crushed the Dubcek government, or is it better now?"

The fellow again said he did not understand, but I noticed he kept glancing over his shoulder at two persons leaning against a wall. The two were gazing at the sky, saying nothing.

Suddenly our friend got up and said he would walk us toward our campsite. Though we weren't ready to go, we followed him. Two hundred yards away he explained: "I could not talk there. They were listening."

"Would you get in trouble if you criticized your government or the Soviet Union?"

Our friend nodded then explained that for such an offense he could be expelled from the university. Forever. Never mind that he lacked only a year completing his academic program. And he would never be allowed to hold many jobs. I then went through a checklist of First Amendment freedoms with our friend. So much for freedom of speech. What about freedom of assembly?

He explained that he secretly meets with a group of students who criticize the government and talk about changes that need to be made. If the government knew of their meetings, harsh measures would be taken. He said they did not even tell one another their names for fear that, if one was caught and pressured, he or she would give the others' names.

And freedom of the press?

My friend looked at me and shook his head. Before the Russians came in 1968 the press was not so restricted. But now the press prints what the government orders. And the government, unlike before, now strictly follows the orders of the Soviet Union.

Freedom of religion?

Our friend said he knew a Christian. One. No, not someone at the university, since Christians were not allowed to attend universities. But he did know a Christian. He did not even mention Jews or other faiths.

I did not think it necessary to ask about the right to "petition the government for a redress of grievances."

When we think about what is right with America, we can look first to the First Amendment. We can look to those most basic freedoms and give thanks.

When I think about what is right with America, I also think about Northern Ireland.

A friend at a Belfast university took me on a short walk near the campus: "Here's a bank the IRA robbed. I think two persons were killed." "Here's the hotel that was bombed this morning," my tour guide explained, as we looked at the rubble being piled outside it.

"And there," he said, pointing to the second floor of a building, "is where my lab class met. On the window up there was part of a postman after a bomb exploded across the street."

Not mere police but military troops patrolled the streets. If they were walking, there were two, each with an automatic weapon, moving back to back. Jeeps always had a driver, another soldier riding "shotgun" with his weapon, and a third soldier in the back with his weapon ready, too.

I went outside the city for a couple of days to a home that enabled mothers and children to escape the violence and the city. The septic line was stopped up, and when they learned I'd worked building sewers for my hometown, they gave me a pair of rubber boots, one of which did not leak, and put me to work. The people were gracious and warm, the children playful and innocent.

In the four days I was in Northern Ireland, four people were killed by sectarian violence. As I looked for the causes of the violence and madness, I found Northern Ireland reminded me of home.

In Belfast Protestants and Roman Catholics live in different neighborhoods. Segregated housing, if you would. Protestants and Catholics go to different schools and attend different churches. People often have different jobs or working places depending upon their religion.

It reminded me of the same America in which I grew up and in which we separated people by race rather than religion.

The reign of God has not been fully realized. Racism is still too prevalent: I wish I had a dollar for every racist remark and joke I've heard recently. But at least in our rural counties here in Northwest Tennessee, black and white children go to the same schools.

Our laws, if not our customs, prohibit racial discrimination in housing and employment. As for our churches, well, the eleven o'clock hour on Sunday mornings continues to be the most segregated hour of the week. But at least it's not quite such an event when I go to preach in a black church or when a black pastor comes to white churches around home. And now, thank God, this does happen.

And when I look to the Philippines, I give thanks for what is right with America. The people voted, and the election was stolen from them, at least until they took it back.

Mind you, Ferdinand Marcos could have learned some of his political techniques from my grandfather, at least according to stories I've heard. I'm told they used to vote at Granddad's country store and prophecies almost were fulfilled: If the dead did not quite rise and walk, they at least voted.

More recently, I worked full time in rural West Tennessee for Al Gore Jr. in his US Senate campaign. If "vote early and vote often" still is the rule here, I found no evidence of it. I'm thankful that today in America our elections generally are free from the wrongdoing of our not-too-distant past and the fraudulent and violent tactics the Philippines suffered.

There's a lot that's right with America. We rightfully can be thankful for our freedoms, for our laws and progress in race relations, and for our election process and the peaceful transitions in government.

And as we give thanks for what is right, we can turn again to address what is wrong.

—"Remembering What Is Right with America,"
Commercial Appeal, 16 March 1986.

Following the Velvet Revolution of late 1980s and the strenuous efforts of Vaclav Havel and other liberalizing leaders, Czechoslovakia was peacefully divided into two independent countries in 1993, the Czech Republic and the Slovak Republic. It is a very different place than when I visited in 1976.

Thankfully, the daily horrors I encountered on my 1976 visit to Northern Ireland were greatly ameliorated by the Good Friday Agreement that

concluded the Northern Ireland peace process of the 1990s. After decades—no, centuries—of struggle over Irish sovereignty and battles between Protestants and Catholics, the Good Friday Agreement addressed
among other things civil and cultural rights, decommissioning weapons,
demilitarization, and justice. Eventually a multiple-party democracy and
a much more peaceful time was born.

Ferdinand Marcos (September 11, 1917–September 28, 1989) was a
Filipino dictator who served as "president" of the Philippines from 1965
until 1986. His regime was notable for nearly unimaginable corruption
and brutality. To protect American military bases in the Philippines, US
Presidents from Johnson to Reagan provided sometimes uneasy support
for his regime.

CHRISTIANS IN EASTERN EUROPE (1979)

In 1976, I received a scholarship to study theology in Europe. Before returning
home, I traveled with my brother and another friend for six weeks in Eastern
Europe. We were especially curious about life for Christians and young people
behind the Iron Curtain.

My hometown is Dresden, Tennessee—named after Dresden, East Germany—so of course we had to go there. In Dresden we found a prayer meeting of about thirty college-aged Christians. They were students at a technical
school. They said they were permitted to learn trade skills, but the government
wouldn't let them go to the university. When we asked them "Why not?" they
replied simply, "Because we are Christians."

We also met an older man in Dresden, a schoolteacher. He said the government prohibited Christians from teaching. But through an oversight, or perhaps
a kind government official, he was still able to teach.

We also traveled to Czechoslovakia. There a university student told us he
knew one Christian—not someone at the university, of course—but one Christian among all of his acquaintances.

I heard that in 1977, a year after we were in Czechoslovakia, another visitor
there remarked: "For me this is living proof that it is impossible—impossible—
to deal with the Communists." That man returned to his native Poland where
he lived and worked for the church. Today he resides in Rome and is known as
Pope John Paul the Second.

When John Paul became Pope, he gave hope to Christians throughout
Eastern Europe. I read that there is now "new life" in the churches there. When

I was there, the churches in East Germany and Czechoslovakia seemed to be almost dead. You might say that they've been resurrected.

Poland was the only country I visited where the church seemed powerful. Today it is even stronger. The *Wall Street Journal* calls the Polish priests "an opposition party" to the Communist government. For instance, the government has banned construction of new churches, but forty churches have been built in recent years. And the government has prohibited religious activities outside authorized churches, but one hundred thousand youths meet in prayer and study groups in homes every week.

In Czechoslovakia, however, the church is still very weak. Many fear it is near death. The Catholic bishops are controlled by the state, and the archbishop, although still independent, is old and sick. Apparently the best hope for a religious revival lies with underground groups of young rebels. Like in the early church, they meet secretly to avoid government persecution.

It's ironic—isn't it? I grew up believing that the government was always right. My father was a judge, and I'm studying to be a lawyer. I've been taught to obey the law. Now I have a friend in Czechoslovakia who breaks the law each time he meets with his Christian friends.

The struggle between church and government was nowhere more symbolic for me than in East Berlin. A huge communications tower dominates the city. It looks something like the Space Needle in Seattle, Washington. It's a tremendously tall, thin concrete structure with a big ball near its top. You can walk around inside the ball with dozens of other tourists and see the entire city. The tower is a showpiece symbolizing modern, technological, and atheistic East Germany. The government sells little replicas of the tower in the souvenir shops.

Almost in the tower's shadow, a few hundred feet away, we found a church, centuries old. During my few days in East Berlin, we had seen the ruins of several churches destroyed in World War II. But this was the only church we'd found open. We walked inside, and there we met three young Christians. Two were daughters of ministers, and all three were studying to become church workers. One noticed the cross I was wearing. She pointed to it and smiled. That was how our friendship began.

We all spent the afternoon together. They told us how the church not only reminded them of the past but how it is also a symbol of hope for their future. And they told us of their hopes for freedom.

The government forbids them from talking about their faith with anyone who isn't a Christian. They hope to be free to do that without fear someday. The government won't let them travel outside Eastern Europe, but they hope someday to be free to come to the West. We talked of their visiting us in the United States. Everyone smiled, but it made me sad. It seemed so hopeless when we were just a few blocks from the Berlin Wall with its concrete and barbed wire. But as my East German friends hoped and dreamed—and believed—their faith helped me believe that it might yet be possible.

I gave my cross to the girl who noticed it when we first met. I told her it could remind her of our shared faith. She put it on and said she would remember. Maybe someday she'll come and give the cross back. I know I'll never forget her and the other Christians we met in Eastern Europe.

Communications towers, the Iron Curtain, and government regulations—they all cast shadows across Eastern European churches. But people of faith survive. And I pray that someday soon they may prosper.

—"Christians in Eastern Europe,"
United Methodist Communications, 1979.

The dreams of my East German friends proved to be well-founded—and they were realized far sooner than most observers thought possible. I'm still shocked that on November 9, 1989, the Berlin Wall fell, and then less than a year later the East German government fell as well. German reunification occurred on October 3, 1990.

Even more shocking was the fall of East Germany's sponsor, the Soviet state, just a little over a year later. While today Russia has fallen under the cruel rule of the KGB's Vladimir Putin, and the people of Russia suffer mightily and too many seeking freedom find death at the government's hands or instigation, my East German friends still give us hope.

JAPAN'S WAR SENTIMENTS UNDERSTANDABLE (2001)

An American Southerner understands that war ends quicker for victors than for losers. Northerners think the Civil War ended in 1865. Southerners know better.

In fact, the war never ended for many of us in the South. We are still fighting battles, still trying to find a way we could have won, still trying to defend our honor and justify our ancestors' actions.

As an American, the war with Japan ended fifty-six years ago, and it seems it is time for the Japanese to "get over it." But as a Southerner I understand why that war haunts Japan even today.

Before coming to Japan, I had read about the textbook and Yasukuni Shrine controversies. But I had no idea that these issues arise so constantly and are matters of such grave concern for many in Japan as well as in the Koreas and China.

When I found myself repeatedly confronted with the Pacific War, I wanted to learn more. So even though Prime Minister Junichiro Koizumi did not go to the Yasukuni Shrine on August 15, I did.

There I found old soldiers, sailors, and pilots gathered. They reminded me of my father's fellow veterans at the American Legion.

These men, both American and Japanese, risked everything and suffered much. They share bonds forged in a crucible I hope my sons never have to know but also a unity that I cannot but envy.

I found young men showing off their black uniforms, trying to march but at times performing like I did as a young Boy Scout not yet skilled in marching.

Some showed off for the cameras, like young men at home will do with rebel flags on their pickup trucks and tattooed on their bodies.[1] Others quietly and sadly remembered loved ones, much the way we Southerners still do near my home at battlefields like Shiloh and Fort Donelson.

At noon, all the people reverently observed a moment of silence, not unlike what we do in the Tennessee Senate in memory of former colleagues when we learn of their passing.

Today I visited a distinguished Japanese leader who was born in 1940. His father went to war in 1941 and did not return until 1945. My friend said he wondered who that man was who came to their house in 1945 and started spending nights with his mother.

This war child gave credit to the United States for providing milk that sustained him, helping him to survive and grow up healthy. Milk in big buckets, poured into individual cups. He thought that the American soldiers (then segregated) were so white skinned because they drank so much milk and even bathed in it.

He said those Americans dressed sharp in their impressive uniforms, smiled all the time, and gave him and his friends chocolate and candy. He is grateful to those soldiers and to the Americans who provided the milk. But then he

---

1   A discussion of the Confederate flag can be found in my memoir of growing up in Tennessee, *Things Held Dear: Soul Stories for My Sons* (Louisville, KY: Westminster John Knox, 1999). See chapter 4, entitled "Growing Up with the Flag."

sighs deeply: "Still that horrible issue is hanging in the air, in our minds. Who started the war? And why, why?"

Those are questions we still wrestle with in the American South even 136 years after the civil war that devastated our homeland. Why, after only fifty-six years, should anyone think that Japan would be through with its painful past?

Similarly, why should the Japanese expect Koreans subjected to thirty-five years of occupation to "get over it"? After all, the US Civil War lasted but four years, then the Northern occupation of the South ended relatively quickly, at least by comparison. Yet, we still talk about Reconstruction as worse than the war itself, cursing "carpetbaggers" and the "Damn Yankees" who came and took advantage of our people in their pain and war-weakened conditions.

Why should any people Japan defeated quieten their voices of concern about what Japan teaches its children? Why should those people not be concerned about the signals that Japan's leading government officials send not only in Japan but across their borders and to their people, too?

As a Southerner, I understand something of defeat and something of the pain that the victor brings. My friend saw American troops bringing candy and milk. But few in other countries remember any war or occupation that way.

I think I understand something of Japan's pain. And I understand why many Japanese want to remember their ancestors, their family, and their friends. But I do not understand why Japanese leaders, leaders of a gifted people so committed to avoiding conflict, have not yet committed to remembering loved ones without causing other peoples to agonize over their lost loved ones—and to fear for their living loved ones.

I understand why the Pacific War has not yet ended. But could there not be at least a cease-fire?

—"Japan's War Sentiments Understandable,"
Japan Times, 15 September 2001, 17.

Unfortunately, this essay may be more relevant today than it was when written. Since it appeared in 2001, there have been continuous controversies across the South and in Tennessee. From Charlottesville, Virginia, to New Orleans, Louisiana, cities have erupted in conflict over Confederate statues. In Charlottesville, a racist drove his car into a crowd and killed a woman.

Closer to home, in Memphis we have seen years of blinding controversy culminating in the night-time raid and removal of the statue of Confederate

General Nathan Bedford Forrest. Confederate Park has been transferred to a nonprofit, and its name has been changed.

In Nashville, Forrest's bust remains outside the doors through which I passed into the House of Representatives and where his legislative defenders and African American legislators still tread beneath his watch. Just this last legislative session, demonstrators protested General Forrest's presence and the official state observance honoring him drew national attention.

Over a century and a half after Lee surrendered at Appomattox, the Civil War is still being fought in Tennessee and across the South.

AN OPEN LETTER TO SENATOR BAKER AND SENATOR SASSER (1981)

[Original Editor's comment:] Roy Herron, a lawyer with West Tennessee Legal Services, had some thoughts about the Reagan administration proposal to quit funding the Legal Services Corporation which provides money to local Legal Services to represent the poor in civil lawsuits. He decided to write an open letter to Sens. Howard Baker and Jim Sasser. It follows:

Dear Senators Baker and Sasser,

I write you because you are fellow lawyers and the leaders of our state's congressional delegation. I write on behalf of more than 660,000 of your constituents who are eligible for assistance from Legal Services. I write as a Legal Services lawyer frustrated by silly accusations solemnly stated and intended to pressure you and your colleagues into denying the poor access to justice.

Legal Services lawyers have been accused of being "radical activists." I confess I've had a liberal education, but a liberal arts degree from Senator Baker's alma mater, the University of Tennessee, hardly makes me a radical. Especially since I attended the Martin campus, not Knoxville, and followed it up with a law degree from Senator Sasser's alma mater, Vanderbilt.

I admit I took money from an international organization to study in a socialist country. But surely taking money from Rotarians to study ethics and New Testament in Scotland does not make me radical beyond redemption.

Last week, however, I read to some "fellow travelers," if you will, the words of our radical leader, a revolutionary executed for threatening the established powers. I repeated and reaffirmed his teachings about nations being judged by how they treat the least fortunate classes.

In my defense, let me stress that I complained to the country church to whom I preached that Jesus's statement in Mathew 25 is awfully radical. That nations will be judged on how we treat the hungry, thirsty, naked, sick, prisoners, and strangers seems too harsh a requirement for salvation. Perhaps a lesser and more reasonable standard would be to judge us on whether we merely provide a few lawyers for the poor?

Patrick Buchanan perhaps anticipated my suggestion when he wrote that Legal Services lawyers are "radical children who believe they have some God-given right to tax dollars to implement their Ideas of social change."

We suffer no illusions about who gives the right to tax dollars—Congress giveth and taketh away—that's why I write you.

Congress also stated our responsibility "to provide equal access to the system of justice in our nation for individuals who seek redress of grievances" who otherwise would be "unable to afford adequate legal counsel."

Though Mr. Buchanan and others accuse us of "trying to implement ideas of social change," 95 percent of my time is spent trying to make the present system work. For example, today a disabled gentleman, nearing seventy, said his disability check and Medicaid card had been stopped and the Social Security Administration was demanding that he pay back over $400.

He allegedly violated a regulation by giving his wife their trailer when she asked him to move out. If they had divorced and the court had awarded her the trailer, everything would have been okay.

"But we don't want a divorce," he said. "She's never had eyes for anyone but me. It's just that since she had that operation, she doesn't want me anymore."

Now one agency won't give him a piece of paper certifying that his Medicaid is cut off, and another agency won't help until he gets the paper. To keep emphysema from choking him and to keep the fluid in his eyes from solidifying and blinding him again, he needs medicines. His only remaining income, a Social Security check, barely covers the cost of the drugs.

"What can I do?" he pleaded. "I can't pay. Can't pay my electric bill or my water bill. Can't make payments on my trailer. What am I going to do, let them take it back next month? Can't buy food. Almost out of medicine and can't pay for that either. How can I live?"

I've arranged for a meeting with agency officials and hope to persuade the system to work voluntarily. If necessary, though, we'll sue.

The man, who never attended the first day of school, is frustrated and weary— as frustrated and weary as I am of being attacked for representing the poor against the government.

I do admit, though, that I also have tried to change the system. My co-conspirators include county officials, juvenile officers, ministers, private citizens, and another legal aid lawyer.

We are trying to create local alternatives for youngsters in trouble. We hope to set up classes providing parent-effectiveness training and teaching how to overcome drug problems. We plan to arrange for college students and young adults to "adopt" juveniles.

We are tired of sending our youth away to state institutions where they learn to become adult offenders. We only seek to enable our own communities to take care of our own children and our own problems. And what is wrong with that social change?

Another charge is that we are, heaven forbid, "idealists." That accusation is accurate. We have been misled by legal ilk such as Oliver Wendell Holmes who urged that lawyers be idealists. It didn't start with Holmes. As James Kilpatrick recently observed, carved above the entrance to the United States Supreme Court are these words: Equal Justice Under Law. "It is an impossible idea, to be sure," Kilpatrick conceded, "but no matter. We ought to strive for the impossible now and then."

Some maintain we must strive for this impossible goal not because we are idealists but because we are realists. One of my New Testament professors pointed out that realism characterizes a biblical view of justice. John Donahue observed that, whether in ancient Israel or modern America, "Injustice is . . . a social cancer which destroys society."

President Nixon, noted more for pragmatism than idealism, recognized this when he introduced legislation creating the Legal Services Corporation. After the turmoil of the sixties and early seventies, he reflected, "We have also learned that justice is served far better and differences are settled more rationally within the system than on the streets."

Historically, much of the impetus for Legal Services came from the American Bar Association and one of its presidents, Lewis Powell, who later was appointed to the Supreme Court by President Nixon.

Bipartisan support created the Legal Services Corporation to remove it from partisan politics. The rights of the poor have been put above political pandering. Until now, the system has worked so well that two Republicans with whom you have served in the Senate recently called the LSC "one of the most successful public efforts for the poor" and "perhaps the single most successful program to emerge from the war on poverty."

Finally, we are called "revolutionaries." To the contrary, we are America's main effort to follow Aristotle's advice on "How to Prevent a Revolution." In his *Politics*, the ancient Greek philosopher wrote: "In all well-tempered governments there is nothing which should be more jealously maintained than the spirit of obedience to law, more especially in small matters; for transgression creeps in unperceived and at last ruins the state, just as the constant recurrence of small expenses in time eats up a fortune."

Legal services lawyers help maintain "the spirit of obedience, more especially in small matters." We serve as law enforcement officers or prosecutors in the civil courts, calling the attention of judges and juries to violations of the civil law.

For example, recently a teenager could not get his landlord to refund a security deposit, despite the fact that he left the premises in better condition than he found it. The manager had pocketed the money and intended to keep it. Instead, a judge awarded my client his $65.

Sixty-five dollars is a lot to someone with less than $67 income per week, the maximum a single person can have and qualify for my program's services. But what really was at stake was more than a few dollars. At stake was a young man's belief in our system of justice, his trust in the ideals taught in school about equal justice and fairness and courts stopping wrongs.

Make no mistake. The denial of representation to the poor will send clear messages. They will know that equal justice under law is a myth. They will know their more affluent fellow citizens care more about saving almost thirty cents a month in taxes than they do about access to justice for the poor.

Senators, when you became attorneys you stood before the Tennessee Supreme Court and swore, "I will never reject, from any consideration personal to myself, the cause of the defenseless or oppressed, or delay anyone's cause for lucre or malice. So help me God."

Sincerely,
Roy Herron

—"An Open Letter,"
The Tennessean, 12 April 1981.

Even indigent citizens accused of crimes have a right to counsel. The US Constitution provides in the Sixth Amendment "the right to a speedy and public trial, by an impartial jury . . . and to have the assistance of counsel for his defense."

In *civil* cases, Legal Services attorneys provide counsel to indigent citizens. Constitutional and legal rights often are meaningless or nullified without an advocate to assert those protections and defend those citizens.

Legal Services attorneys today continue to assist and represent impoverished citizens, though this program has suffered substantial cuts and remains under repeated attacks even now.

2
RELIGIOUS LIBERTY

In 1997, Representative Craig Fitzhugh and I sponsored and the General Assembly passed the Tennessee Student Religious Liberty Act. This law set forth clearly the religious liberty and free speech rights of public-school students. It protected students' rights to pray, discuss their religion, observe religious holidays, and bring religious texts to school.

In 2008, Representative Mark Maddox and I sponsored and the General Assembly approved the Bible in Schools Act. This law enabled the Bible to be taught in public schools in a constitutional way and required the state to approve a curriculum for a course of non-sectarian, academic study of the Bible.

Following are op-eds written to defend this legislation.

PROTECTING STUDENTS' RELIGIOUS LIBERTY (1998)

A Tennessee fifth grader is told he cannot bring his Bible to school, because that would "violate the separation of church and state." Another child is instructed not to mention God in a school essay, for the same reason.

A school chorus is advised not to perform a song that includes the word

"God." A pupil assigned to paint what she likes about spring is told her poster of Jesus at Easter is "too religious."

Such all-too-common incidents, reported by teachers and attorneys throughout the state, have caused many Tennesseans to conclude that God has been expelled from public schools and that the US Supreme Court has outlawed school prayer.

In fact, the high court has *not* prohibited all voluntary prayer in public schools. Yet some well-meaning educators—who, like most of the rest of us, are uncertain or misinformed about this confusing area—continue to deny students religious liberty and free speech.

After decades of struggle, these issues have not gone away; if anything, the battle grows more intense. The stakes are steadily mounting for public schools, their students, the Constitution, and all of us who believe in the rule of law and the value of freedom.

Government should not dictate our children's prayers or beliefs. But neither should government schools dictate that our children cannot pray and must abandon their beliefs. The Constitution does not require government hostility to religion.

Some in Washington say we need a new constitutional amendment, so students someday can pray again in schools. Rather, citizens need to demand that existing constitutional rights be honored now.

As country humorist "Cotton" Ivy said: "It ain't what Cuckleburr don't know that worries his teachers; it's what he knows that just ain't so!"

What imperils our children's religious freedom is not the lack of a constitutional amendment. For two centuries, our First Amendment has been the greatest constitutional provision and protection in human history.

What imperils our children instead is what we know that just isn't so.

The First Amendment's establishment clause does not prohibit prayer in public schools, although many think the Supreme Court has ruled that it does. The amendment's free-exercise clause protects religious liberty; its free-speech provision protects religious speech.

We should quit believing the misstatements, myths, and outright lies, whether from extremists on the far left who wish school prayer would go away or extremists on the far right who wish public schools would.

Both ends of the political spectrum have become so accustomed to raising money and memberships by promising to protect each from the other that neither soon will consent to tone down the rhetoric. Those focused on talking about their "enemies," rather than listening to and working with them, often profit from continued warfare—at the expense of the rest of us and the peril of our children. When we listen to one another and work together, though, consensus can emerge.

We sponsored the Tennessee Student Religious Liberty Act, which recently took effect. The law expresses the religious liberty and free speech rights of public-school students. It is designed to prevent government discrimination against religion and to see that students' existing constitutional rights are honored.

In preparing the legislation, we listened to members of diverse groups: from the Christian Coalition to Jewish Community Centers, from the American Civil Liberties Union to pastors in our districts. We worked with students, teachers, school boards, superintendents, and their attorneys.

Consulting leading religious liberty lawyers and the Tennessee attorney general, we developed legislation to prohibit discrimination against students of faith. Over many months, we built a consensus. Not one of these diverse groups opposed the final measure.

The legislation is simple, yet we are told no other state has done so much as Tennessee to protect the religious freedom of its schoolchildren.

The law provides that, to the same extent and under the same circumstances as students are permitted to communicate nonreligious views, possess and distribute nonreligious literature, or be absent for nonreligious reasons, public school students may voluntarily pray—silently or out loud, alone or with others.

They may express religious viewpoints. They may speak to and attempt to share such viewpoints. They may possess and distribute religious literature. They may be absent for religious holidays or practices.

If students are allowed to talk about Michael Jordan and the Bulls during recess, they can talk about Jesus Christ and the Baptists, or Abraham and the Jews, or whatever their own religious beliefs may include.

If students can talk to their teacher at lunch, they also can pray to their Teacher. If they can talk with one another about things secular, they can pray with one another about things sacred. If students can carry secular books to school, they can carry their Good Book.

However, they may not infringe on a school's rights to maintain order and discipline, to prevent disruption of education, and to determine curriculum and assignments. They may not harass others or coerce others to participate in their activities. They may not infringe on others' rights.

And the law specifically prohibits government employees violating the First Amendment's establishment clause by directing religious or anti-religious activity.

Citizens should know the truth about the religious liberty and free speech rights of students in public schools. Religious students should not be discriminated against.

Some people fear that religious freedom can be abused and that knowledge of legal rights can be dangerous. For two hundred years, though, America's perilous yet wise path has been to choose freedom over oppression and knowledge over ignorance. Armed with knowledge and blessed with freedom, America can and will do right.

We need not wait for another constitutional amendment to protect religious liberty; we need to use the one we have. The new Student Religious Liberty Act gives us the statutory tools to do exactly that.

—Co-authored with Representative Craig Fitzhugh.
"Protecting Students' Religious Liberty,"
Commercial Appeal, 1 March 1998.

Twenty years later, my concerns about the extremes making it impossible to turn down the rhetoric about religious liberty or the lack thereof have, sadly, turned out to be prescient. The US Supreme Court continues to be a battleground for those seeking to expand or restrict religious liberty and free speech rights.

TEACH STUDENTS ABOUT BIBLE SO THEY CAN BETTER UNDERSTAND WORLD (2008)

Last year, *Time* magazine on its cover proclaimed, "Why We Should Teach the Bible in Public Schools." The story acknowledged the Bible as "the most influential book ever written."

Yet, half of American adults cannot name the first book of the Bible, or even one Gospel. Respected pollster George Gallup called us "a nation of Biblical illiterates."

Worse yet, our young people are becoming the most Biblically illiterate generation in American history. Too few students know classics in the Bible, such as Psalm 23, the Sermon on the Mount, or First Corinthians 13.

Furthermore, too many students have no idea that numerous literary classics quote Scripture, build on Biblical themes, and convey Biblical teachings. As Union University Dean Gene Fant has pointed out, the examples in literature include Shakespeare's *Macbeth*, Milton's *Paradise Lost*, and countless others.

Too many American history students do not understand the Biblical allusions in Abraham Lincoln's second inaugural address, such as, "It may seem strange that any men should dare to ask a just God's assistance in wringing their bread from the sweat of other men's faces, but let us judge not, that we be not judged."

Too few recognize the Biblical references in Benjamin Franklin's words to the Constitutional Convention: "We have been assured, Sir, in the Sacred Writings, that 'except the Lord build the House, they labor in vain that build it' . . . without His concurring aid we shall succeed in the political building no better than the builders of Babel."

Too many art students do not appreciate the meaning of Michelangelo's Sistine Chapel, Rembrandt's *Return of the Prodigal Son* or DaVinci's *Madonna of the Rocks*. Too many music students do not know the Biblical references in Handel's *Messiah* or Aaron Copeland's *Appalachian Spring* symphony.

If young people do not understand the importance and impact of the Bible on literature, music, and art, in history and culture, where do they get their values and visions? The television wasteland? Internet temptations? So much musical mess? In our coarsening culture, why not let students learn about and from the world's best-selling book?

Yet, in more than 80 percent of Tennessee's counties, not even a single high school offers a Bible course. Only four counties in Middle Tennessee and two in West Tennessee have schools offering a Bible course. Why? One reason is that school administrators and school boards fear being sued.

The Bible in Schools Act that we sponsor asks the state Board of Education to create a curriculum so that local schools can offer Bible courses without being sued. This course will be designed by expert educators and approved by leading lawyers.

Not everyone loves this bill. On that, the far right and the far left agree. They both wish this legislation would go away.

The far left fears violating the First Amendment's Establishment Clause through government-mandated religion. But this bill does not force a single county, school, teacher or student to participate in this optional, elective curriculum.

The far right fears violating the First Amendment's Free Exercise Clause through a government-mandated curriculum. But our law did not eliminate, alter, or disturb a single Bible course already being taught.

Instead, this bill seeks the teaching of our sacred Scripture in a way that honors our sacred Constitution. Our government schoolteachers cannot constitutionally *preach* the Bible, but they can *teach* the Bible.

In 2008, the author and Representative Mark Maddox sponsored
the Bible in Schools Act enabling the Bible to be taught in public
schools in a constitutional way. The author and Charlie Daniel were
"on the same page of the hymnal." Illustration by Charlie Daniel,
Knoxville News Sentinel.

The same *Time* magazine that recommended teaching the Bible in public
schools advised doing so "very, very carefully." This bill does that by providing
that the course be a "non-sectarian, non-religious academic study of the Bible."

The bill prohibits attempts to indoctrinate students, to teach religious
doctrine, or to disparage or encourage commitment to any particular set of
religious beliefs.

This bill is a common-sense proposal that Tennessee's attorney general
has recognized as constitutional, even commending the bill for going to

PRINCIPAL SMITHERS, SOME STUDENTS WANT TO TALK TO YOU ABOUT BRINGING THEIR RELIGION INTO TENNESSEE SCHOOLS.

In 1997, the author and Representative Craig Fitzhugh led a bipartisan effort to protect student religious liberty and free speech. Cartoonist Bruce Plante had some fun pointing out that the Student Religious Liberty Act would protect every student's freedom. Illustration by Bruce Plante, *Chattanooga Times*.

"considerable lengths in order to comply with Supreme Court opinions on religious materials in public schools."

That being so, why not allow students to study history's greatest book and understand how it has changed our world? Then maybe those Biblically literate young people will go out and change their world.

—Co-authored with Representative Mark Maddox.
"Teach Students About Bible So They Can Better Understand World,"
Jackson Sun, 11 March 2008.

PART 2. LIFE

3
PUBLIC SAFETY

In this section are essays about legislation meant to keep Tennesseans from harm and to save lives. The first essay opposes a bill that would encourage beer joints and bars to sell more alcohol to intoxicated customers who become the drunk drivers who harm or kill.

The second essay argues for legislation to protect more babies and youngsters through car safety seats.

The third essay opposes legislation that would have repealed Tennessee's law requiring motorcycle riders to wear helmets.

The fourth essay decries needless deaths caused by Tennessee's lack of interstate safety barriers between opposing lanes.

The last essay concerns the Tennessee Children's Product Safety Act to prohibit the manufacturing, distributing, or selling of unsafe children's products.

LIQUOR BILL PUTS LIVES IN GOVERNOR'S HANDS (1986)

Dear Governor Alexander,

I write to you on behalf of victims and potential victims of drunk drivers.

No one has appointed me a spokesman, but the deaths of five friends because of drunken driving compels me to write.

A bill that may create new victims and that will deny compensation to other victims has passed the General Assembly and awaits your decision on whether to veto it. I'm talking about the bill that would encourage beer joints and bars to sell more alcohol to intoxicated customers and that would prevent innocent people injured by those drunken customers from being compensated.

Governor, I'm sure my characterization of this bill is not identical to that of liquor lobbyist Tom Hensley, "the Golden Goose." Nor would those lobbyists representing the other big businesses selling alcohol talk about their pet bill this way.

After all, the legislation is full of legal jargon such as "proximate cause" and "beyond a reasonable doubt." But let's cut through the legalese and talk about the practical effects, the real impact of this legislation.

Judy is about thirty-five years old. She previously worked in a factory. She was the type of person you brag about when you talk about why the Saturn plant came to Tennessee—a hard worker with Tennessee values.

Last fall while she was driving alone, an oncoming car swerved across the center line and struck her car head-on.

Judy was more fortunate than many struck by a drunk driver; she lived. But she still suffered injuries to her head and knee and severe cervical strain.

Today, Judy still limps, and the pain in her neck and the headaches continue. A physician I know treated Judy and referred her to a specialist. Both doctors are conservative, respected physicians not prone to exaggeration. This week one reported: "Essentially her injuries are permanent. . . . After five months recuperating, with essentially permanent disability, she is unable to carry on her previous livelihood."

And you, Governor, now have the power to decide whether others like Judy have any hope of compensation for medical bills, lost wages, and disability.

You see, the drunk fellow who drove into her car is poor and uninsured. If she sues him, she'll get nothing because he has no assets and no insurance.

Under current law, if she sues the bar that served the beer and helped the man get too drunk to drive, she has a chance of being compensated for her expenses and injuries. Under the bill on your desk, however, people in her situation would find it almost impossible to gain relief. They would have to prove by a tougher criminal-law standard ("beyond a reasonable doubt") rather than the current and appropriate civil standard ("preponderance of the evidence") that the sale was "the proximate cause" of the injury or death and that the sale was "to an obviously intoxicated person" and that the person caused the injury or death as "the direct result of the consumption of the alcoholic beverage or beer so sold."

It is hard to understand why the General Assembly would mess up our laws any further by inserting a criminal law standard into civil law to protect alcohol sellers. This bill creates a wall so high and a moat so wide that almost no one, no matter how innocent and horribly injured, can gain compensation from any alcohol seller, no matter how negligent and irresponsible.

But don't just take my word for it. Listen to one of our Tennessee state troopers. When I asked a veteran trooper what he thought about the bill, he told me, "It's difficult enough now to prove that a driver was drunk and got drunk at a particular place. The people selling beer and alcohol don't feel enough responsibility now. They don't assume the responsibility they should to stop serving drunken persons anyway. We sure don't need to make them any less responsible."

Furthermore, if that bill becomes law, the highway patrolman told me, "The victims will be the ones that have to pay the bills. The innocent ones that get run over by drunks and are crippled, disabled—they're the ones that'll have no relief."

While Judy was still in the hospital, less than three miles down the same stretch of road, two young people were killed. The car in which they rode was rear-ended by a car driven by a man who had gotten drunk in two beer joints.

Only a few months earlier on the same three-mile stretch of road, another woman and her three children were injured in a head-on collision. Another drunk driver drove into the innocent family right after leaving the same place that served Judy's drunk driver. In less than a year on less than three miles of road, these three wrecks injured five innocent people and killed two youngsters—and the drunken drivers all got drunk in beer joints.

Maybe, in the cities, more affluent killers come out of the fancy bars in the plush hotels that have lobbied for this bill, but out here in the country most of the drunk drivers come out of what we call "beer joints" or just "joints." In all three crashes, the drunk drivers did *not* have insurance. If the victims or their families are to be compensated, it will have to be by the establishments that sold beer to the drunk drivers.

But isn't this an unusual coincidence? Hardly. In fact, a state trooper friend told me, "A huge percentage of the ones drinking and coming out of the joints and causing wrecks have no insurance because of prior DUIs." Their licenses have been revoked, or they are high-risk drivers who will not or cannot pay the expensive insurance premiums.

The state trooper, an accident reconstruction specialist, reported that at least half of the fatal accidents involve alcohol. Of those drinking drivers, "a real high majority come out of some joint."

Governor, you probably read this week that the National Traffic Safety Administration reported that states raising the legal minimum drinking age saved seven hundred lives in 1984. Tennessee was one of those states, and you were our governor when the drinking age was raised.

Furthermore, our tougher DUI law apparently has saved lives, too. That legislation also became law while you have been governor. You have helped save lives before.

The question now, however, is whether you are going to weaken the law holding alcohol sellers accountable for serving alcohol to intoxicated persons.

Governor, you often talk about "Tennessee values." Well, most Tennesseans value the lives of our loved ones too dearly to increase the risk any traveler faces every time he or she drives down the road.

We also would value a governor standing up to the liquor lobby and telling them you will not provide special protection for wrongdoing.

Those selling alcohol can protect their pocketbooks by not serving drunken customers.

And you can protect the lives of innocent and law-abiding Tennesseans by responsibly and rightfully vetoing this special-interest bill.

Grace and peace,
Roy Herron

—"Liquor Bill Puts Lives in Governor's Hands,"
Jackson Sun, 9 March 1986.

Unfortunately, Governor Alexander did *not* veto the legislation, and it remains the law today.

Extremely skilled attorneys like my late Senate colleague Mike Faulk still sometimes successfully brought cases for innocent victims. But many, many times those who have been harmed cannot prevail when jurors are required to apply the criminal law "beyond a reasonable doubt" standard in judging the civil liability of the joint that kept selling to a drunk until he wove drunkenly away.

We have made progress in other ways. The presumption of intoxication at 0.10 was lowered to 0.08.[1]

State troopers today tell me drunk drivers still kill too many. But they also note that the increasing and current challenges often involve prescription drugs, other drugs, and "distracted driving."

Legislation to hold the negligent and reckless accountable and to compensate victims remains a desperate need. And stopping businesses from gaining immunity or near immunity so they can profit even more from their negligent and reckless acts and avoid accountability for the harm they inflict on others is more a challenge now than ever.

Drunk-driving was an ongoing concern for both cartoonist Charlie Daniel and for the author, who sponsored tougher blood alcohol content standards, mandatory ignition interlock devices, and other anti-drunk-driving legislation. Illustrations by Charlie Daniel, *Knoxville News Sentinel*.

---

1 *Tennessee Code Annotated* 55–10–401(a)(2): "The alcohol concentration in the person's blood or breath is eight-hundredths of one percent (.08 %) or more." For our youngest drivers, a tougher and tighter standard of 0.02 now applies. See also, *Tennessee Code Annotated* 55–10–415(a)(2): "A person under twenty-one (21) years of age shall not drive or be in physical control of an automobile or other motor-driven vehicle while . . . the alcohol concentration in the person's blood or breath is two-hundredths of one percent (0.02%) or more."

SAFE BABIES OR HIGHWAY CARNAGE (1989)

In 1987, eighteen children under four died on Tennessee highways. Sixteen of those were not properly protected by safety seats. In 1988, another eighteen children under four died on state highways. Fifteen of those also were not protected as required by law.

Five of those thirty-six infants and toddlers died in child safety seats because the accidents simply were not survivable. But almost all the thirty-one other little ones would have lived if they had been protected in safety seats.

In January, Tennessee legislators held eight public hearings on our current law. More than twenty legislators heard testimony calling for substantial changes.

Dr. Michael Decker, a physician in preventive medicine at Vanderbilt University Medical Center, has studied how to save children from injuries and death. He told legislators that children are eleven times more likely to survive a serious accident if they are in child safety seats.

Dr. Allen Anderson, a pediatric surgeon at the University of Tennessee Medical Center, testified on a national study estimating that, for every child killed in a car wreck, another seventeen are permanently disabled. When that study is applied to Tennessee, last year car wrecks permanently disabled more than three hundred Tennessee toddlers and infants.

Dr. Anderson reported that 85 percent of the small children who die in wrecks die from head injuries. Most of the children left permanently disabled are disabled by injuries to the brain.

In 1977, Tennessee passed the first child restraint device law in the country. In Dr. Decker's phrase: "We were the leaders; now we're the laggards."

A recent nineteen-city study by the National Highway Traffic Safety Administration found that 84 percent of children under four were protected by child safety seats. But the Tennessee Department of Health and Environment reports that only 39 percent of our children are being protected.

Is it that we love our children less than half as much? Of course not. But in Tennessee two fundamental problems have stopped us from increasing usage of safety seats: poor enforcement and poor distribution.

Enforcement has lagged for three reasons: (1) local law enforcement agencies and governments are not doing what they might; (2) too many courts are not taking the offenses seriously enough; and (3) punishment options for courts are too limited.

While Tennessee troopers last year issued a record number of citations, most local law enforcement authorities issued few or none. The most recent data on disposition of citations issued by troopers reveal that 83 percent did not result in conviction. Even for those 17 percent who were convicted and presumably punished, the maximum punishment was $10 and no court costs.

Fines should be increased. Courts and clerks should not be asked to handle the cases without costs. Taxpayers should not be asked to subsidize the handling of these cases.

The second major problem is the distribution of child safety seats. The solution can be found in our hospitals.

All but 200 of the 66,000 babies born in Tennessee each year arrive in hospitals. It is the only place where we know trained and caring health professionals and educators are together with parents and infants. Many hospitals already help protect newborns. Vanderbilt and Donelson hospitals give seats to all newborns. In Chattanooga about 3,500 leave the Erlanger Hospital protected by child safety seats. The same is true in Clarksville and Huntingdon.

If hospitals purchased the seats in bulk, parents could save about half of what it would cost them otherwise. Parents who can't afford the seats could be provided for in a number of ways. If we are serious about wide distribution of safety seats, the hospitals must help see the child's first ride is a safe one.

Literally almost a child a day either is killed or permanently disabled because he or she wasn't protected. We Tennesseans love our children too much to let such carnage continue.

We led the country before in protecting our children. We can do it again.

—"Safe Babies or Highway Carnage,"
The Tennessean, 6 March 1989.

The bill eventually passed, but only after attacks and struggles. One lobbying organization opposed requiring hospitals to distribute safety seats to new parents. Eventually hospitals were required to educate parents about this law, tell them where they can buy a safety seat, and make sure babies left the hospitals in safety seats.

In addition to requiring safety seats for children under four, colleagues and I sponsored legislation in 1995 that required children under twelve to wear seat belts. In 2003, we made child restraint requirements even stronger.[2]

---

2   1995 *Tennessee Public Acts*, Chapter 112: Protecting Children by Safety Belts; 2003 *Tennessee Public Acts*, Chapter 299: Expanding protection of young children through greater safety restraint system requirements.

The author and Charlie Daniel both worked to protect
Tennesseans on our highways. The author sponsored
child safety seat legislation and fought for safety
barriers along our interstates. Illustration by Charlie
Daniel, *Knoxville News Sentinel.*

HELMETS OFF RIDERS, BRAINS ON PAVEMENT (2007)

The General Assembly is deciding whether to repeal our motorcycle helmet
law. Many riders like to feel the wind in their hair. Some want the freedom to
decide whether to wear a helmet.

But allowing wind in the hair will mean heads hitting pavement. Allowing
the freedom to ride without helmets means some will lose the freedom to work
or walk or think.

The Insurance Institute for Highway Safety reports:

* The risk of dying per mile traveled on a motorcycle is 34 times that
  of in a car.
* Even as other roadway deaths declined, motorcycle deaths more than
  doubled between 1997 and 2005.

* The National Highway Traffic Safety Administration (NHTSA) reports helmets reduce the likelihood of dying in a motorcycle crash by 37 percent.
* In a crash, unhelmeted motorcyclists are three times more likely to suffer traumatic brain injuries.

The director of the Trauma Center at Vanderbilt University Medical Center, Dr. John Morris, flatly states, "Having cared for hundreds of injured motorcyclists, it's painfully clear that helmets save brains and lives."

Other states have suffered

But what has happened in states that have repealed their helmet laws?

Texas has been down this road twice. When Texas weakened its law to exempt adult riders, fatalities jumped 35 percent. Texas reinstated its law for all motorcyclists and saw serious injuries reduced. It later weakened its law again, requiring helmets only for riders under twenty-one. In the first full year after that change, fatalities increased 31 percent.

Arkansas weakened its law and saw fatalities increase by 21 percent. When Florida exempted riders twenty-one and older, the death rate rose 25 percent.

NHTSA reported that twenty-five (yes, twenty-five!) studies of the costs of motorcycle injuries "consistently found that helmet use reduced the fatality rate, probability and severity of head injuries, cost of medical treatment, length of hospital stay, necessity for special medical treatments, and probability of long-term disability."

It is not easy to wash our hands of responsibilities or burdens. Those trying to follow Biblical teachings are called to love our neighbors and be our brother's keeper. Injuries too often burden taxpayers.

The medical research is clear. That is why Tennessee doctors, hospitals, and trauma centers oppose repealing our helmet law.

The scientific studies are clear. That is why insurance entities and governmental agencies oppose repeal.

The real world experience is clear. That is why state troopers and other law enforcement officers oppose repeal.

Tennessee can save lives, bodies, and brains, as well as insurance costs and tax dollars, by saving our motorcycle helmet law. Wind in the hair is not worth brains on the pavement.

—"Helmets off Riders, Brains on Pavement,"
The Tennessean, 18 April 2007.

The author and Charlie Daniel both opposed legislation to repeal the requirement that motorcycle riders wear helmets. They both wanted to keep motorcyclists' brains off the pavement and save them from becoming road kill. Illustration by Charlie Daniel, *Knoxville News Sentinel.*

Despite years of attempts to repeal Tennessee's motorcycle helmet law, so far legislators have continued to protect Tennesseans and refused to pass repeal. This is so despite thirty-one states now failing to protect their citizens with universal helmet laws, including our Kentucky and Arkansas neighbors who require helmets only for younger riders.[3]

CABLES OR CROSSES: INTERSTATE SAFETY BARRIERS (2012)

A couple of weeks ago in West Tennessee, a wreck on Interstate 40 killed three men. If our state government had acted, they might have lived.

---

3   "Motorcycles," Insurance Institute for Highway Safety, last modified May 2019, https://www.iihs.org/topics/motorcycles#helmet-laws.

A tire on the pickup truck the men were riding in blew, sending the westbound truck hurtling across the median into an eighteen-wheeler that was heading east. A simple safety barrier in the median could have saved the three men.

Crossover crashes are far more dangerous than other types of traffic accidents. In an examination of 135,198 crashes on divided highways in California, the National Transportation Safety Board found that crossover wrecks were more than five times deadlier than non-crossover accidents. In North Carolina in 2006, interstate crossover crashes alone caused 32 percent of the traffic fatalities.

When two vehicles traveling 70 miles per hour approach each other and collide, the closing speed of 140 miles per hour often makes escape impossible and death inevitable.

Construction of safety barriers in the median strips of Tennessee's interstate highways would drastically reduce the number of such deaths. The state Department of Transportation has erected some median safety barriers, and those already have saved lives. But too many still are dying—life after life, death after death.

Last February 29, one of us was at a store off Interstate 40 in West Tennessee when there was a horrible crash. A car had slammed into a truck, sending it into the median, where no barrier stopped, slowed, or deflected it from continuing into the opposing lanes of traffic and hitting another eighteen-wheeler. Nothing could be done for the two people who died, including the driver of the third vehicle, who was incinerated in the fire that erupted.

Liz LaVelle was the twenty-year-old daughter of Dr. David and Jenny LaVelle of Shelby County. Two years ago, Liz was driving from Memphis back to her beloved Lipscomb University. On I-40 near the Fayette County-Shelby County line, her car crossed the median and was struck by a westbound eighteen-wheeler. Literally thousands mourned the passing of this incredible young woman.

A few years before that tragedy, another amazing young woman of deep faith also drove I-40 for the last time. Mary Margaret Pilcher was the daughter of Atha and Jim Pilcher of Fayette County. At eighteen, she also was a faithful, lovely student, a high school senior. On Valentine's Day in 2004, as she drove from Jackson toward her family's home in Somerville, a vehicle headed in the opposite direction crossed the median, became airborne, landed on her vehicle, and killed her.

All these who have died in West Tennessee on I-40 represent many more victims. In fact, we recently looked at a federal government map showing the locations of fatal cross-median interstate crashes involving large trucks. Interstate 40 from Memphis to Nashville and Interstate 24 from Chattanooga to Clarksville appear to have had as many or perhaps even more fatalities per mile as any other stretch of interstate highway in the US. In Tennessee in 2010, crossover crashes averaged a fatality a week, according to the state Department of Safety.

This year the General Assembly passed legislation requiring law enforcement agencies to report whether safety barriers are present at accident sites. But knowing more is not doing more. Other states are far ahead of us in the construction of lifesaving safety barriers. And it is hard to explain to grieving Tennesseans why we don't do as much as our neighbors in Missouri, South Carolina, and many other states to protect citizens and save children.

Missouri has 680 miles of median safety barriers on its interstates, more than twice as many as Tennessee, which has but 284.8 miles of cable barriers on its 1,104 miles of interstate highway. And Missouri is adding an additional 120 miles of barriers, more than the 93.9 miles of barriers we have on the entire 190 miles of interstate highway in West Tennessee.

South Carolina, a fourth smaller in geographic area than Tennessee, has a fourth more interstate median safety barriers. To be equivalent, we would have to install over 250 miles of median safety barriers.

The Tennessee Commissioner of Transportation rightly says that saving lives is our top transportation priority. That being so, we believe the department should immediately erect safety barriers on interstates everywhere they can save lives. We should not wait for more to die to identify where barriers are needed. The department must be proactive and prevent deaths, rather than reactive and count deaths.

Governor Bill Haslam is pro-life. His family business serves millions of motorists and truckers, so he knows well the dangers on the interstates. We are fortunate that he is exactly the right governor at the right time to save countless lives. And he has commissioners of transportation and safety who also want to help him save lives. Together they can stop the carnage of interstate crossover crashes.

The solution to saving lives and saving families from needless and unspeakable pain is simple. These safety barriers are the difference between life and death. In the words of Deuteronomy 30, we should "choose life, that both you and your children might live."

—Co-authored with Rachel Rodriguez.
"Cables or Crosses: Interstate Safety Barriers,"
Commercial Appeal, 18 August 2012.

Over seven years later, Tennessee still lacks hundreds of miles of interstate safety barriers.

Since this essay was written, on Interstate 40 in West Tennessee a former Shelby County Republican Party Chairman and Assistant Commissioner in the Haslam Administration named Bill Giannini died needlessly. His vehicle crossed the interstate median, and he was killed. A safety barrier would have saved him. He is perhaps the most prominent recent victim, but in the seven years since this essay was written, many more have died on Tennessee's interstates in cross-median fatal crashes.

BOOST FEDERAL INSPECTIONS BEFORE WORSE INCIDENTS HAPPEN (2007)

Pigs, this week. The *New York Times* reported Thursday, "A highly infectious swine virus is sweeping China's pig population . . . creating fears of a global pandemic."

Last week, toys and toothpaste. In recent weeks, fish and medicine for humans, and even food for pets.

Not only are imports at record levels, but so are dangers from poisonous products that our children play with and we put on our toothbrushes and dinner plates.

How much toothpaste sweetened with poisonous antifreeze, how many antibiotics infected with bacteria, how many sick fish, how many pets poisoned, and how many children's toys painted with lead does it take before serious action is taken? Particularly since quality control in some countries appears to be limited to occasionally executing a particularly corrupt official.

Representative Sherry Jones and I are sponsoring a bill to ban sale of unsafe children's products in Tennessee and hope for passage in the next legislative session. But the Constitution and federal law limit much state action. So, our federal friends need to act. President Bush has, finally, appointed a panel to look at this dangerous situation, but the emphasis on doing it with "existing resources" could cripple attempts to protect our families.

Imports are four times what they were a decade ago, yet inspector staff levels at the Food and Drug Administration have fallen to 2002 levels. Last year, those inspectors looked only at 20,662 imported shipments out of 8.9 million. No, they don't have to look at every shipment, but checking 20,000 and letting 8.9 million come uninspected hardly inspires confidence or provides safety.

Why couldn't those countries selling products here bear the expense of additional and needed inspections? Free trade and fair trade are not necessarily the same. And imports should not be free from the reasonable cost of protecting Americans.

A friend who was an executive with a clothing manufacturing company that not long ago employed more than five thousand people in West Tennessee and Western Kentucky explained it this way: "We went to Mexico because we could hire a Mexican for a week for what we paid a Tennessean for a day. And then we went to the Far East because we could hire someone there for what we paid a Mexican for a day."

That means the worker in the Far East is paid less in a week than what Tennesseans make in two hours. Now that company is gone and no longer employs even a single Tennessean.

Sometimes that old adage applies: "You often get what you pay for." In many countries, they don't pay for decent wages, more expensive lead-free paint, or costly but crucial inspections of food and medicines. They don't pay for clean air or water—then send us the polluted, contaminated fish and food.

It is time not just for free trade but for fair trade and for clean food, safe drugs, and unpoisoned products.

—"Boost Federal Inspections Before Worse Incidents Happen,"
The Tennessean, 17 August 2007.

Unfortunately, this bill did not pass.

As Tennessee waited for the federal government to intervene and protect our children, we have seen more recently the federal government also fail repeatedly to protect children, not only in this area, but also, for example, in places like Flint, Michigan, with lead-poisoned drinking water.

4
PUBLIC HEALTH

The first of the following essays advocates helping schools while discouraging smoking by taxing cigarettes at a rate closer to the national average.

The next essay advocates for the Tennessee Non-Smoker Protection Act that has prohibited smoking in public places such as restaurants, schools, hotel lobbies, and shopping malls, protected thousands of Tennesseans who would have died from others' smoking, and helped many smokers cut back and quit.

The third essay advocates for the federal Affordable Care Act that helps hundreds of thousands of Tennesseans.

The fourth essay decries a federal government bureaucracy outrageously attempting to stop a conscientious family physician from serving his patients.

BIG TOBACCO IS SELLING MISLEADING MYTHS (2007)

The thirteen-year-old found his father unconscious on the floor. The cardiologist told the man's almost-widow that if he didn't quit smoking three packs of Camels a day, he would not live to see his boys grow up.

The twenty-three-year-old was in Nashville when his mother called. His father had gone to feed the cattle, but a neighbor found him near the grain bin. Decades of smoking had taken their final toll.

The fifty-one-year-old held his sister's hand, then sat beside her bed and watched her last emphysema- and lung cancer-tortured breath.

I was that boy and that young man. I am that brother. Cigarettes killed my father and my sister. For that reason, and for the sake of all of Tennessee's children, I support Governor Phil Bredesen's Schools First proposal funded by raising our cigarette tax, the fourth-lowest cigarette tax in the nation.

But the governor's Schools First plan is obscured by a cloud of smoke—misinformation from Big Tobacco. The governor recently said, "I frankly think a lot of [the misinformation] is being driven by tobacco company lobbyists," adding he'd heard Big Tobacco's talking points recited repeatedly. Here's what Big Tobacco's telling:

Myth No. 1: "Tennessee's got plenty of money to fund new education investments." Unfortunately, we rank forty-fifth in funding schools. Even if the cigarette tax money and as much of the revenue growth as possible go into education, our children will still receive less than students in nine-tenths of other states. But $200 million would help at-risk kids in rural and urban schools and suburban taxpayers trying to pay for fast-growing schools.

Myth No. 2: "Raising the cigarette tax to sixty cents a pack is too much." Bull feathers. The governor's proposal would put Tennessee's cigarette taxes barely above *half* the national average of $1.02.

Myth No. 3: "This money isn't going to schools but to the general fund." Sadly misleading. We always fund education through the General Fund, our state's main checking account. In any event, the governor is fine with setting aside new dollars for schools.

Myth No. 4: "The cigarette tax isn't a stable revenue source." Unfortunately, untrue. With so many addicted to cigarettes, and cigarette companies spending billions to addict more, declines in usage will be painfully—and deadly—slow. State fiscal projections are conservative and account for gradual declines in smoking.

Myth No. 5: "Raising the cigarette tax is doing taxpayers wrong." Wrong again. Increasing the cost of cigarettes will help some adults stop smoking and stop a lot of kids from starting. This will save taxpayers from spending so many millions on TennCare, health insurance for teachers and state and local government employees, and many of the costs of cancer, lung disease, and heart disease. That is pro-taxpayer and anti-tax.

Bottom line: If we raise the cigarette tax to barely more than half the national average, some adults will quit smoking, some teens won't start, taxpayers will pay less for the health care of addicted victims of cancer and heart and lung disease, and our children can have better schools. Don't let the cigarette companies blow smoke in your eyes—or harm any more of our children.

—"Big Tobacco Is Selling Misleading Myths,"
The Tennessean, 15 April 2007.

Senate Bill 2326/House Bill 2354 passed the House on a vote of 59 to 35. With a constitutional majority requiring 50 votes, the vote was close enough to cause concern. But that was a "landslide" compared to the final vote in the Senate of 17 to 16. The bill became Public Chapter 368 of the Public Acts of 2007 on June 19, 2007.

FRONT LINES OF THE SMOKING WAR (2007)

Because of my father and my sister, the governor's bill to ban smoking in the workplace that I sponsored in the Tennessee Senate was personal for me. It is also painfully personal for many of you. But this issue is both personal to Tennesseans and part of a national battle to save lives.

From Maine to Washington to California to Florida, states are protecting their people through smoke-free workplaces. But it's not just states on our country's corners, not just blue states on the borders. It's industrial states like Ohio and Illinois; rural, property-protecting places like South Dakota, Idaho, Montana, Nevada, New Mexico, and Utah; and Southern states like Arkansas, Florida, and Georgia. And this year in Tennessee, our Democratic governor joined those Republican neighbors in providing bipartisan leadership to protect Americans.

Giving workers clean air to breathe, that does not give them cancer, emphysema, and heart attacks, is pro-worker. That's why workers' organizations supported this bill.

Protecting businesses from litigation involving workers' compensation, disability benefits, unemployment compensation, handicap discrimination, retaliation and wrongful discharge, class-action lawsuits, and soaring health-care costs is pro-business. That's why the Tennessee Chamber of Commerce and the Tennessee Restaurant Association supported this bill.

Being pro-taxpayer means reducing the $614 tax burden from smoking-caused government expenditures that the average Tennessee family bears every

In 2006, the General Assembly prohibited smoking in state buildings. Supporters of the legislation joined Governor Phil Bredesen for the bill signing. At the left in front and in blue is Josephine Binkley, who for a quarter-century was the author's amazing legislative assistant and his boss. Also there were Senator Diane Black, Representative John Hood, Senator Mark Norris, and prime sponsors Representative Craig Fitzhugh and the author. Others present included representatives of the Tennessee Medical Association, the Tennessee Hospital Association, and other pro-health organizations. Photo: State of Tennessee Photographic Services.

year. It means fighting to save taxpayers from spending billions and billions on TennCare, Medicaid, Cover Tennessee, state employee health insurance, local government health insurance, teachers' health insurance, university employees' health insurance, and subsidies to hospitals—from Chattanooga's Erlanger to Memphis's Regional Medical Center, which we call The Med. All of these suffer the enormous costs of smoking-related cancer, lung disease, and heart disease. That's why three out of four Tennessee taxpayers support this new law.

Saving Tennessee's 1,740 adults, children, and babies who die each year from other people's smoking is pro-life. Saving the 9,500 Tennesseans that die each year from their own smoking is pro-life. Saving the 132,000 children now alive in Tennessee that otherwise will die prematurely from smoking is pro-life.

Protecting babies in the womb and mamas and daddies from the tomb is pro-life. That is why Tennessee's hospitals, doctors, nurses, pharmacists, and other health professionals supported this bill.

Charlie Daniel and the author teamed up again, this time to protect state workers
and citizens visiting their state buildings from secondhand smoke. For two decades,
the author was unable to pass anything to discourage smoking, not even restrictions
on teachers smoking in schools. Finally, Representative Craig Fitzhugh got the
House to pass a bill prohibiting smoking in state buildings, and the author got the
bill through the Senate. Illustration by Charlie Daniel, *Knoxville News Sentinel.*

This year the General Assembly did something that is pro-worker, pro-
business, pro-taxpayer, and pro-life. We passed a workplace-smoking ban, and
now this law will save you money and save Tennessee lives.

We did not take this action to punish smokers. Believe me, having watched
my sister battle her addiction to the cigarettes and nicotine even as she battled
emphysema and lung cancer, I have nothing but sympathy and concern for
smokers.

Your General Assembly and governor acted to help smokers quit, help young
people not start, and help everyone avoid the unintended but awful consequences of secondhand cigarette smoke.

—"Front Lines of the Smoking War,"
The Tennessean, 7 October 2007.

The year after prohibiting smoking in state buildings, Representative Craig Fitzhugh and the author again teamed up with Governor Bredesen, as well as allies across the aisle like Senator Jim Tracy, future Congressman Tim Burchett, and future Lieutenant Governor Randy McNally. Their legislation made Tennessee the first tobacco-growing state to outlaw smoking in public places. Crucial to the success were the American Cancer Society, the American Heart Association, the American Lung Association, the Tennessee Restaurant Association (led by restauranteur Randy Rayburn), and other advocates for public health and for workers. In this cartoon, Charlie Daniel applauded—at least so the author chooses to think. Illustration by Charlie Daniel, *Knoxville News Sentinel.*

WHY DOES THE GOP HATE HEALTH CARE PLAN? (2013)

Republicans in Congress hate the Affordable Care Act. Some hate "Obamacare" so much that last week they shut down the federal government in a failed attempt to delay implementation.

So, what is it about the Affordable Care Act that Republicans hate so much?

Is it the fact that the last Republican nominee for president, the former governor of Massachusetts, fathered "Obamacare" at the state level? Would Republicans like the Affordable Care Act better if it were called, as it could be, "Romneycare"?

Is the Republican hate for the Affordable Care Act because insurance companies are facing increased competition on prices, giving consumers a better deal?

Is it that consumers now have more low-cost options and can make an apples-to-apples comparison of insurance plans?

Is it that women no longer can be discriminated against and charged higher premiums just because they are women?

Is it that cancer victims and those suffering from a multitude of illnesses no longer can be denied care because of "pre-existing conditions"?

Is it that citizens can get free preventive care?

Or is it that seniors now are saving hundreds of dollars on prescription drugs?

Is it that young people can be covered by their parents' insurance until they are twenty-six?

Is it that some now will have access to affordable care and no longer have to ride on the backs of the rest of us? Is it that many previously uninsured will pay an affordable premium instead of shifting the cost of an unexpected hospital bill onto us taxpayers and insurance-buyers?

Is it that now health insurance is required, just like car insurance?

Is it that insurance companies no longer get huge windfalls and businesses and consumers now get refunds and rebates?

Is it that your insurance company no longer can cap your coverage if you suffer an awful, chronic disease or a costly, debilitating accident? Furthermore, is it that if you suffer such a terrible fate, the insurance company cannot kick you off the insurance altogether?

Is it that working people now can have health care just like the politicians and the prisoners?

Is it that health care inflation has slowed and health care costs have increased less since the Affordable Care Act passed than in any other four-year period since World War II?

Is it that more Americans having health insurance will mean that each year literally thousands fewer will die prematurely from inadequate or delayed care?

Is it that "death panels" never existed and still don't?

Is it that, instead of crashing the economy, the Affordable Care Act is providing healthier workers who strengthen businesses and increase productivity?

Is it that the Congressional Budget Office reports that the Affordable Care Act is a fully funded program that actually helps shrink the deficit?

Is it that many Republicans think that, if people are helped by the Affordable Care Act, they will like it and support it?

Is it that, for the first time in American history, many working people will be able to have what every Republican member of Congress has: affordable health insurance?

Or have the Republicans been yelling so long that they don't know what it is they don't like about the Affordable Care Act, except when they call it by the president's name?

One thing is for sure. When the Affordable Care Act is fully implemented, if it works as well for all Americans as it does for Governor Mitt Romney's home-state citizens, Republicans won't call it "Obamacare" anymore.

I wonder if they'll call it "Republicare"?

—"Why Does the GOP Hate Health Care Plan?"
The Tennessean, 12 October 2013.

The Affordable Care Act was passed in 2010. In that fall's elections, many Democratic candidates for Congress were defeated, in part because the Republicans attacked the Affordable Care Act and labeled it "Obamacare" and it became unpopular with many voters.

From 2011 through 2018, when Republican majorities set the agenda and called up legislation in the US House of Representatives, they voted over seventy times to repeal the Affordable Care Act.[1]

In 2017, the Republican majority in the US Senate came within a single vote of going along with the Republican House in approving the repeal of the Affordable Care Act, but three Republican senators voted against repeal, including the cancer-stricken and dying Senator John McCain.[2]

In 2018, many Democrats and some Republicans promised to keep Americans' protections against insurance companies refusing to issue or canceling their health insurance because of "pre-existing conditions." And many analysts reported that issue was decisive in races that delivered the majority of Congressional seats to Democrats.

---

1   Chris Riotta, "GOP Aims to Kill Obamacare Yet Again after Failing 70 Times," *Newsweek*, 29 July 2017, https://www.newsweek.com/gop-health-care-bill-repeal-and-replace-70-failed -attempts-643832.

2   Peter W. Stevenson, "The Iconic Thumbs-Down Vote That Summed Up John McCain's Career," *Washington Post*, 27 August 2018, https://www.washingtonpost.com/politics/2018 /08/27/iconic-thumbs-down-vote-that-summed-up-john-mccains-career/.

In 2019, the President continued to denounce the deceased Senator McCain for voting against repealing the Affordable Care Act, and most states with Republican attorneys general continued to challenge the Act in court.

It appears that the worst thing for the Republicans politically will be if the courts ultimately rule for them and strike down the protections for pre-existing conditions and the other protections listed above. Millions of Americans depend on our health insurance as protected by the Affordable Care Act, and they will be devastated by the destruction of the ACA. It is hard to imagine that there will not be a corrective political backlash against those who took away their protections and kept them from affording health care for their families.

WHY IS "BIG GOVERNMENT" FIRING OUR SMALL-TOWN DOC? (2014)

The Trump administration is using an Obama administration regulation to give a well-respected, highly trusted West Tennessee doctor a professional death sentence. This is the worst abuse of an individual by Big Government I have ever seen.[3]

Dr. Bryan Merrick of McKenzie has selflessly practiced medicine here for thirty years. He has more than four thousand patients in Carroll, Henry, and Weakley Counties.

He makes house calls and even treats patients in his home. He gives his cell number to fragile patients so they can reach him day or night.

The night McKenzie Mayor Jill Holland's father died, Dr. Merrick made yet another house call to help her father in his last hours. Without Dr. Merrick, Mayor Holland says her father never would have made it to ninety-eight.

Why is Dr. Merrick's career in jeopardy?

Last April, the Centers for Medicare and Medicaid Services revoked his Medicare privileges, accusing him of Medicare fraud after finding that over a twenty-month period ten of his patients had been incorrectly billed.

Dr. Merrick acknowledges the billing errors, but the records show they were clerical mistakes made by others. In some cases, nursing home or hospital

---

3   I wrote this for and with the stories of Mayor Jill Holland of McKenzie, Tennessee. This essay has been edited to reflect that.

clerks wrote down the wrong patients' names. In others, Medicare asked him to review case files, but Medicare failed to notify him the patients had died.

Out of more than 30,000 billings, Medicare found 30 incorrect billings. That is less than one clerical mistake in every 1,000 billings—less than one-tenth of 1 percent. The total incorrect billings amount to less than $1,000, or less than $1.40 a day.

Looked at another way, the staffs at the clinic, nursing home, and hospital where Dr. Merrick works got it right more than 99.9 percent of the time. At the school where my children went, that's an A-plus, but for the same score Dr. Merrick is being professionally expelled.

Dr. Merrick, who is appealing the revocation, was the medical director of the nursing home and the only internist at the McKenzie hospital.

He is the primary physician for more than two thousand local Medicare patients. He is their lifeline. Many already have said they won't change doctors. That includes the Mayor's eighty-five-year-old mother.

What will happen to them? They do not have months and years to wait on hearings and an appeals process that may take years.

Scientific studies in medical journals show that taking a physician away from elderly patients results in more hospitalizations and, yes, more deaths.

Last week Mayor Holland joined with Huntingdon Mayor Dale Kelley, McLemoresville Mayor Phil Williams, Carroll County Mayor Kenny McBride, and Bethel University President Walter Butler in meeting with US Representative David Kustoff.

They also have reached out to Senator Lamar Alexander who chairs the Senate health committee and Senator Bob Corker who also is highly respected.

They would not have done that if they thought Dr. Merrick had done anything wrong. Some of these seniors will die if our elected federal officials don't step up and help.

The only fraud being committed here is the federal government claiming Dr. Merrick committed fraud.

The only abuse here is the federal government abusing thousands of patients who are about to lose their beloved doctor in a region the federal government has designated as at-risk and underserved.

—"Why Is 'Big Government' Firing Our Small-Town Doc?"
Commercial Appeal, 24 October 2014.

Dr. Bryan Merrick continued to serve his Medicare patients without charging for his care while he tried to get his Medicare billing rights restored.

McKenzie Mayor Jill Holland led efforts to get the federal bureaucracy to look at the facts. As Dr. Merrick's attorney, I accompanied him to Washington, DC, to meet with members of Congress and their staffs. On another trip, Dr. Merrick and I went to Baltimore to meet with the responsible federal officials.

Finally, after nine months of struggles, four law firms, countless calls and meetings, and expenses and lost revenues totaling hundreds of thousands of dollars, Dr. Merrick finally prevailed. Today he again is allowed to serve Medicare patients without federal harassment.

As chairman of the TennCare Oversight Committee and later as chairman of the Senate Health and Human Services Committee, the author met countless times with physicians, nurses, and other caregivers. Photo: Dean Dixon.

5
HEALTH CARE FOR WORKERS
TENNCARE

When Tennessee's Medicaid program struggled with soaring costs swallowing the state budget, Governor Ned McWherter proposed an innovative and extraordinary change to a managed care system. Governor McWherter called this new version of Tennessee's Medicaid program "TennCare."

TennCare was controversial and under attack from its beginning. After Governor Sundquist's Administration struggled to manage the program, radical changes were proposed to take health insurance from thousands of Tennesseans. These two essays responded to those proposals.

SLASHING TENNCARE IS NOT THE ANSWER (1999)

TennCare absolutely needs reform. But stashing funds from TennCare, which is what some advocates of "fixing" the program have in mind, would not solve Tennessee's budget problems. To the contrary, it would make them worse.

Despite what some critics claim, TennCare has saved Tennessee taxpayers hundreds of millions of dollars and is a major part of any budget solution.

Since 1993, spending on TennCare (which replaced Tennessee's Medicaid program) has grown much less than the average rate of Medicaid spending in other Southern states. If TennCare had grown at the average regional rate, that would have cost us another $200 million in state tax dollars this year alone.

TennCare spent less per recipient in 1997 (less than $2,100) than the state's Medicaid program spent in 1992 (about $2,200). TennCare costs us $1,000 less for each recipient than what other Southern states spend each year on their Medicaid clients.

Sure, total state spending on TennCare has increased as health care costs have gone up and as federal matching funds, which are pegged to a state's per-person income, have declined. But the latter development reflects our state's growing prosperity—surely something that no one would wish away.

Some "reformers" would cut TennCare spending by denying health insurance to more than five hundred thousand citizens who do not qualify for Medicaid. These are working people who cannot afford health insurance and uninsurable patients who have suffered catastrophic illnesses.

More than a third of these people are children. Nearly three-fourths live below the poverty level. Those above the poverty level pay premiums to TennCare that we use to collect federal matching dollars.

Denying insurance to these people could initially reduce the TennCare budget by almost $1 billion, as critics claim. But it would save the state only $323 million, since we would lose nearly $650 million in federal matching funds.

And the half-million Tennesseans dropped from the TennCare rolls still would have health care needs. Those denied prenatal, preventive, or early care would come to hospital emergency rooms when they are very sick. They would seek care at the worst stages of their illnesses and require the most costly treatment.

The hospitals that treat these citizens would suffer additional uncompensated costs, creating greater financial stresses. More of these struggling hospitals would fall, especially in rural and inner-city areas.

If the state then tried to help those hospitals, as we have done in the past, we would have to provide charity care with fewer federal matching dollars. The cost of this alone could exceed the TennCare "savings." And cost shifting by these hospitals would tax those of us with health insurance by raising our premiums, again without the help of federal matching funds.

Slashing TennCare would increase the stress and mortality rate of hospitals that already must cope with federal Medicare cuts. Five Tennessee hospitals have closed in the past thirteen months. Last year, 43 percent of Tennessee's hospitals lost money.

Doctors and other health care providers would get even less compensation. Those who continued to serve TennCare patients would be treated less fairly.

More likely, TennCare providers, who are too few already, would quit. Inadequate provider networks would weaken further.

TennCare's managed care organizations would struggle even more. Some might go under, as the managed care company Xantus already has done. Management of TennCare would not improve but likely would deteriorate because of the increased challenges posed by decreased funds.

Others would "fix" TennCare by cutting patient benefits. But a recent actuarial study by an independent accounting firm concluded that TennCare benefits are "substantially similar" to those provided by Medicaid programs in nearby states.

The auditors indicated that cutting TennCare benefits would yield only small savings. And again, even those savings would disappear when children and disabled adults without private insurance need care, but cannot pay for it out of pocket, and when providers are not compensated for that care with federal matching funds.

The TennCare Partners program that is supposed to serve the addicted and mentally ill already has gutted efforts to fight alcohol and drug addiction. Cutting TennCare would make it even more anemic and inadequate. More people who need care would not get it. Local governments would have still more mentally ill and addicted persons in their jails, and the state would have still more in our prison—all at taxpayer expense and without federal funds.

You'd have more human tragedies like the mentally ill woman—whose behavioral health organization (BHO) said she was not sick enough to warrant pay for her care—who then killed her children and herself. Like the young man who was forced out of a mental hospital after three days because that was all his BHO would pay for, even though his doctor said he needed more care. He killed his father.

Bashing TennCare and destroying hospitals and health care are not the changes the program needs. The next "permanent" director of TennCare will be the eighth person to hold that title in five years. Getting the right director, who can and will stay to manage the program, is crucial. The recent appointment of John Tighe to oversee the program is a strong first step.

The Sundquist administration has recognized the need for, and acted to provide, stable, appropriate funding. Another part of the solution is a "pay or play" bill that would prevent insurers and employers from dumping their sickest, most expensive policyholders and workers on TennCare.

Reform TennCare? Of course. But take away health insurance from children, disabled and catastrophically ill people, and the 160,000 former welfare recipients and members of their families who are working and fighting to stay off welfare?

Force hospitals all over Tennessee to close? Discourage medical providers from serving our fellow citizens? Push more managed care organizations into bankruptcy?

We think not. We pray not.

—Co-authored with Representative Page Walley.
"Slashing TennCare Is Not the Answer,"
Commercial Appeal, 21 November 1999.

QUESTION: CAN TENNCARE BE SAVED IN ITS CURRENT FORM? YES (2000)

TennCare can and will be saved. It has broad support, and its market-based fundamentals are sound.

TennCare has transferred the purchasing power of Medicaid dollars to the private sector to allow firms to use the program's large number of enrollees and market forces to obtain the best prices.

But to go from government controls to a free-enterprise system is never easy or pretty, as many in Eastern Europe can testify. TennCare has encountered the problems facing every state's health-care system: general health-care inflation, soaring pharmaceutical costs, floundering managed-care organizations, hospitals hammered by Medicare cuts, some insurers and employers dumping the sick from plans. The Bureau of TennCare itself has struggled, as would any agency with seven directors in five years.

Yes, improvements are needed. For instance, employers and insurers must be stopped from dumping sick workers on the state. The administration must attract and retain the needed personnel like Deputy Commissioner John Tighe, who heads the program. The state must make sure there are adequately capitalized and funded managed-care organizations so providers can and will serve patients.

Yet after six years in operation, here's what TennCare has provided:

- Coverage for five hundred thousand citizens who previously had no insurance—at a cost that is $1,000 per person lower than the southeastern average for Medicaid patients.
- Improved health care for chronically ill adults who are now able to work and support themselves.
- Former welfare recipients who were totally dependent on government and working uninsured who were dependent on charity care now are paying premiums.
- There is less cost-shifting to businesses and those with private insurance.
- There is less burden on Tennessee taxpayers.

This is why diverse groups, from hospitals and physicians to managed-care organizations and businesses, testified last week before the TennCare Oversight Committee that TennCare must continue.

It's also why Governor Don Sundquist has insisted that TennCare be strengthened and sustained. Mr. Sundquist, a Republican, has bipartisan support in a Democratically controlled legislature that knows the good TennCare has done.

Without TennCare, five hundred thousand individuals, many of them children, would be left without coverage. Many enrollees are small business owners or people who work for small businesses, and they can't afford insurance on their own. Others have worked their way off welfare but still cannot afford health insurance.

Some critics have said that TennCare, with its funding problems, is putting a big financial burden on hospitals. But without the program, hospitals will incur an even greater financial strain because they would be forced to care for people on a charity basis, with no compensation at all. Also, costs would be shifted to businesses and citizens with private health insurance.

Others have charged that TennCare's enrollment is out of control. But in fact, enrollment is near where it was five years ago. And it hasn't even kept pace with the population growth. The slight rise is due to the state's successful efforts to cover uninsured children. In addition, at the Legislature's urging, the bureau has increased verification of eligibility to be sure only those who qualify participate.

Sometimes private management fails, and companies fail with it. We have seen that with one managed-care organization. But some have served the public well and have made money doing so. Those that have been struggling should get a boost with the increased funding to place TennCare on an actuarily sound basis.

Sometimes companies bargain very hard and we certainly have seen that with BlueCross BlueShield. Analysts believe the financial interests of BlueCross and the state will ensure the continuation of this mutually beneficial relationship.

As our nation grapples with the challenge of covering forty-four million uninsured Americans, TennCare can continue to teach Washington policy makers that there is much to learn from federalism's "laboratory of the states."

—"Question: Can TennCare Be Saved In Its Current Form? Yes,"
Wall Street Journal, Southeast Journal, 2 February 2000.

TennCare continues today, having saved Tennessee taxpayers literally billions of tax dollars and having saved families literally thousands of lives. TennCare struggled throughout the Sundquist Administration with constant turnover and disruption as it went through nine directors in eight years.

TennCare's leadership was strengthened and stability finally achieved under the strong and selfless leadership of longtime public servants Darren Gordon and Dr. Wendy Long. Gordon served ten years as Director and was first aided and then succeeded by Dr. Long, who served eight years as medical director and then three years as Director of TennCare. Dr. Long in turn was aided by Gabe Roberts, who served six years as chief counsel and chief operating officer and then succeeded Dr. Long as Director in 2019.

All three of these public servants—Darren Gordon, Wendy Long, and Gabe Roberts—certainly could have made more and probably could have worked less in the private sector. But their able leadership and faithful stewardship together with the selfless service of many others addressed countless challenges and made a huge difference in the management of the program and in the services to millions of Tennesseans.

In Governor McWherter's last legislative session, he proposed to radically reform Tennessee's Medicaid program, calling his proposal "TennCare." The initial "sputtering" reaction by interest groups and legislators is captured here. Illustration by Charlie Daniel, *Knoxville News Sentinel*.

6

HEALTH CARE FOR WORKERS

MEDICAID EXPANSION

In recent years, nearly three-fourths of the states have expanded their Medicaid programs by accepting almost total federal funding. Fourteen states, including Tennessee, so far have refused to help their citizens get health care with these federal funds. The following essays argue for expanding Medicaid and allowing hundreds of thousands of working Tennesseans to purchase health insurance for their families.

WORKING PEOPLE NEED STATE TO ACCEPT FEDERAL FUNDS, EXPAND MEDICAID (2013)

Brain cancer attacked Virginia's husband. At the end, when he couldn't take any more, the thirty-three-year-old took his own life. As did her son at nineteen. A year ago her home was burgled. Then she got behind on her house payments.

For thirty-one years, she's worked at the same restaurant. In addition, three days a week, she also works at a nursing home, trying to make enough to save her Knoxville home.

No benefits.

No health insurance.

In Nashville, near the Capitol, in a small, inexpensive restaurant, one

71

extremely nice and polite waiter always hustles to serve us all. No matter when I go, he is there. I finally asked how.

Tim explained he works from 10 a.m. until 11 p.m., thirteen hours a day, seven days a week. That comes to ninety-one hours a week.

On a good day, he makes $100. There aren't enough good days.

No benefits.

No health insurance.

Then there's Linda. Once or twice a week, she serves me breakfast at the family-owned restaurant in Nashville where she's worked nineteen years, ten hours a day, six days a week.

Ten years ago, within sight of her home, her son was killed in a car wreck. Five years ago, cancer killed her husband. And took her health insurance.

The cheapest health insurance Linda could find was $2,000 a month. Her paycheck barely covers her mortgage; tips sometimes cover everything else. There's sure not $24,000 a year for health insurance.

Restaurant servers are only one group of working people needing health-care security. Others include the self-employed, many construction workers, temporary staff, clerks, workers in small businesses, and even employees of the world's largest, most profitable retailer.

Which Tennesseans need expanded Medicaid for health insurance?

Not unemployed single mothers and their young children—they have TennCare health insurance.

Not retired senior citizens—they have Medicare health insurance.

Not convicted felons in prison or murderers on death row—we already pay for their health care.

Not the politicians—the governor and his family, the commissioners and their families, the legislators and their families, members of Congress and their families. All these politicians have access to government health insurance.

But what about working people? The Tennesseans without health insurance are working people.

So, if the politicians and the prisoners, the lawmakers and the lawbreakers, have government-provided health care, what's wrong with working women and working men having health care?

Folks like the Nashville waiter and the Nashville and Knoxville waitresses.

Many states are accepting federal funds to provide health care for working citizens near the poverty line. Tennessee has not.

Turning down 100 percent federal funding for three years to expand Medicaid means our federal tax dollars will be sent as far as California and New York and as close as Kentucky and Arkansas. We will fund all the states choosing to enable health care for working citizens.

Some 330,000 Tennesseans in working families—including 80,000 children—could qualify for the federal government paying the full cost of their health care for three years. After the three years, we could opt out if we didn't want to pay, at most, 10 percent.

Will Tennessee accept the federal funding to expand Medicaid coverage to include working people?

Unless our Republican governor—like nine other Republican governors—and Republicans in the Legislature act, Tennesseans will pay taxes for other states to get health care, but our working women and men will do without.

No benefits.

No health insurance.

The public servers are depending on the public servants. The waitresses and the waiters and many other workers are waiting to see.

May they wait no more.

—"Working People Need State to Accept Federal Funds, Expand Medicaid,"
Knoxville News Sentinel, 4 August 2013.

EXPANDING MEDICAID IS TO CHOOSE LIFE (2013)

At thirteen, I found my father on the floor. He'd had a heart attack.

What passed for an ambulance back then in rural Tennessee rushed him to the hospital.

The doctor told Mother if Dad had gotten to the hospital ten minutes later, the doctor could not have saved him.

If the hospital had not been there, the doctor could not have saved him.

Now that hospital—like many others—is at risk. More than fifty hospitals in Tennessee are struggling financially, and we are told that some will close.

And when hospitals close, other children's fathers and other loved ones will die.

Why is this happening? Because the Republican officeholders controlling this state have refused to cash a federal check.

Tennessee could extend health insurance coverage to as many as 330,000 people in working families if state officials accept the federal funds that would pay 100 percent of the costs of expanding the state's Medicaid program for the first three years.

And if, but only if, we wanted to continue the expansion beyond three years, Tennessee would not have to pay more than ten cents on the dollar. Hospitals providing millions of dollars in uncompensated care to uninsured patients could be paid for their services and stay open.

But so far, Tennessee's Republican governor and Republican legislators have refused to accept $1 billion a year of federal funding to cover 330,000 working poor. This is money that hospitals, doctors, and nurses need to serve patients in rural areas and even in urban centers such as Nashville, where at least one major hospital is now releasing hundreds of employees.

The *New England Journal of Medicine* last year published research dealing with "Mortality and Access to Care" that documents how access to health care saves lives. The study, conducted by researchers from Harvard's School of Public Health, analyzed data from states that did and states that did not expand their Medicaid programs to cover low-income adults without children or disabilities.

The researchers found that, when more people have access to health care, more people live—"particularly those between the ages of 35 and 64 years, minorities, and those living in poorer areas."

In fact, they found that for every 500,000 adults included in state Medicaid programs, deaths declined by 6.1 percent. In other words, Medicaid expansion for 500,000 saved about 2,840 lives per year.

In the words of the study: "This finding suggests that 176 additional adults would need to be covered by Medicaid in order to prevent one death per year."

Officials say 180,000 more Tennesseans could receive Medicaid coverage next year if the state accepts the federal funding. If they are not served, according to the Harvard study, more than 1,000 could die.

Deuteronomy 30:19 recounts Moses proclaiming God's Word: "I have set before you life and death, the blessing and the curse; therefore choose life that you and your children may live."

None of our neighbors and loved ones should have to die because politicians rejected Deuteronomy 30 and the Golden Rule.

Any Republicans denying Tennesseans lifesaving health care ought never again call themselves "pro-life," not if they condemn thousands of uninsured Tennesseans to die.

Fortunately, there is still time to choose life. Pray that they will.

—"Expanding Medicaid Is to Choose Life,"
Commercial Appeal, 8 August 2013.

REPUBLICANS' STAND ON MEDICAID WILL BE DISASTROUS FOR LOCAL HOSPITALS (2013)

Recently, a Tennessee Republican leader said he opposes extending health insurance coverage to 330,000 Tennesseans: "It's kind of like when my daughter says, 'Hey Dad, we need to buy this dress, because it's 50 percent off.' It's just the other 50 percent I have to come up with."

He's a good dad, and he's right about dresses, but on Medicaid expansion, he is 50 percent off and 100 percent wrong.

The accurate analogy is, "It's kind of like when my daughter says, 'Hey Dad, we need to buy this dress because it's 100 percent off.' It's just the zero percent I have to come up with."

The first three years of Medicaid expansion—to extend health coverage to 330,000 working people—are paid for with 100 percent federal funds. And even if we choose to continue in the fourth year and beyond, the cost is capped at ten cents on the dollar.

Extending Medicaid will bring one billion federal dollars a year into Tennessee communities. Payments to hospitals and clinics will then go to doctors, nurses, administrative staff, janitors, medical suppliers, X-ray technicians, therapists, groundskeepers, nurses' aides, cafeteria workers, secretaries, administrators, executives, information technologists, clerks, and even counselors and chaplains. They in turn will spend their paychecks on goods and services, creating more jobs.

Study after study confirms that federal Medicaid dollars spur enormous economic activity. A University of Memphis study concluded that Medicaid expansion in Tennessee would produce eighteen thousand new jobs.

Our Republican lieutenant governor admitted refusing the $1 billion "is going to hurt. In some cases there may be hospitals that have to close. But look, if you want to operate in a free market, things like that happen."

The only problem is that my friend the lieutenant governor is blaming our free market for his governmental decision. Denying hospitals federal funds is not a free-market decision—it's a political decision by this Republican administration and Republican legislature.

Similarly, the Republican House Speaker told reporters last spring, "There are some rural hospitals that will be hurt; there's no doubt about that. But the health care industry is a changing industry, and those that can't keep up, they just simply can't."

That's like pulling the oxygen mask off a struggling patient and then saying,

"That's life—and death—in the free market. If you can't keep up, if you can't keep breathing, then just die."

It's not just a question of keeping up. My friend the House Speaker, instead of blaming hospitals for not keeping up, should accept responsibility for denying hospitals federal funding. The Speaker also said, "If [the prediction of hospitals struggling] was a little exaggerated, we'll find out in the next six months."

Four months later, Vanderbilt University Medical Center is cutting one thousand jobs. Vanderbilt attributes the loss of hundreds of these jobs to the growing cost of uninsured care and the failure to expand Medicaid.

It's not just a Nashville problem. Within forty miles of my West Tennessee home, two hospitals are closing and converting into a "clinic" and "emergency center," and at least two more hospitals are firing employees.

Almost half of Tennessee's general medical and surgical hospitals have been losing money or have survived only with disappearing federal support. These fifty-four especially vulnerable hospitals employ more than 21,000 Tennesseans and support the jobs—and care—of tens of thousands more.

How many hospitals have to close? How many Tennesseans have to be fired? How many lives have to be lost?

The hospitals at risk serve both Republicans and Democrats. The workers and the patients at risk are both Republicans and Democrats. But whether the hospitals and the patients survive is up to our Republican governor and Republican legislators.

This ought not be a partisan issue. It ought to be about saving hospitals, savings jobs, and saving lives.

—"Republicans' Stand on Medicaid Will Be Disastrous for Local Hospitals,"
The Tennessean, 24 August 2013.

Unfortunately, too many hospitals have closed and more still are at risk. Among those closing in recent years:

2013
Starr Regional Medical Center, Etowah

2014
Gibson General Hospital, Trenton
Humboldt General Hospital, Humboldt
Haywood Park Community Hospital, Brownsville

2015
United Regional Medical Center, Manchester
Parkridge West Hospital, Jasper

2016
Tennova Healthcare-McNairy Regional, Selmer

2017
Copper Basin Medical Center, Copperhill

2018
McKenzie Regional Hospital, McKenzie

2019
Takoma Regional Hospital, Greeneville
Cumberland River Hospital, Celina
Jamestown Regional Medical Center, Jamestown

2020
Decatur County General Hospital, Decaturville[1]

WHY TENNESSEE SHOULD EXPAND MEDICAID (2013)

If you have health insurance, why should you care that Governor Bill Haslam and Republican legislators have refused federal funds to insure 330,000 working Tennesseans?

Because their decision will have major consequences for you.

Here are 10 reasons you should care whether 330,000 Tennesseans get health insurance or don't.

1. The rejection of a billion dollars a year will severely impact caregivers. Hospitals near you may close, cut services, or fire workers, as at least four hospitals near my rural Tennessee home have done.
2. Without the hospital, your doctor may move, and other doctors won't come to a county without a hospital, leaving you with fewer options and farther to drive for care.
3. Without a hospital or doctors, companies will not move to your county or may leave, taking jobs from you, your family, and friends.

---

1 According to *Becker's Hospital Review*, consulting firm Guidehouse reported another nineteen rural hospitals in Tennessee "at high risk of closing." That somber analysis was *before* the COVID-19 pandemic and the economic downturn.

4. In an emergency, how many of your family or friends may not survive a longer trip to lifesaving care from a hospital or doctor?

5. You may have to attend more funerals because denying people access to reliable health care costs lives. Applying a recent *New England Journal of Medicine* study[2] Tennessee indicates expanding Medicaid coverage, in the first year alone, would save more than one thousand Tennesseans.

6. If federal funds aren't spent, your city and county will collect less in sales taxes, putting more pressure on local governments to raise your property taxes.

7. Similarly, your city and county may collect less property taxes from for-profit hospitals and from doctors and employers who leave, again forcing your taxes up.

8. Even if your hospital survives, your neighbor, your family member, or even you may lose your job, like the one thousand health-care workers that even Vanderbilt University Medical Center is letting go. Or you may lose your job because others lose their jobs and don't have money to spend with the business where you work.

9. Because of staffing cuts, you may wait longer when you go to the doctor, nurse, or hospital.

10. Your insurance premiums will be higher due to hospitals shifting the cost of care for those without health insurance to those of us with health insurance.

A University of Memphis study projected that the Affordable Care Act would reduce uncompensated care and bad debt by $2.3 billion a year in Tennessee. That's $2.3 billion of cost that will be dumped onto insured patients through increased premiums. Without Medicaid expansion, this cost shifting will continue to drive up premiums for people with insurance by more than $1,000 a year for some insured families.

Furthermore, you and your family will be denied the insurance savings that consumers are seeing in states where officials accepted the funds to provide basic health insurance for low-income families.

Recently New York insurance regulators approved rates averaging at least 50 percent lower than those currently available. Beginning next month, individuals

---

2 B. D. Sommers, K. Baicker, and A. M. Epstein, "Mortality and Access to Care among Adults after State Medicaid Expansions," *New England Journal of Medicine* 367, no. 11 (2012): 1025–34.

now paying $1,000 a month or more for coverage will pay as little as $308. For some, federal subsidies will lower the cost even more.

USA Today reported, "In the 25 states that have decided to expand Medicaid, 12.4 million uninsured Americans will be eligible to pay less than $100 a month."

In states where officials refused the Medicaid expansion, like Tennessee, citizens will miss out on these dramatic savings.

Refusing to take the federal funds and not insuring Tennesseans shifts costs to those of us with health insurance. Call it a "sick tax" or an "uninsured tax," but whatever you call it, refusing the 100 percent federal funds will cost those of us with insurance more as we are forced to pay for the care of families without insurance.

—"Why Tennessee Should Expand Medicaid,"
Chattanooga Times Free Press, 10 October 2013.

The author said in many speeches, "If the politicians and the prisoners, the lawmakers and the lawbreakers, have government-provided health care, what's wrong with government helping working men and women get health care?" Charlie Daniel made the same point, but more powerfully. Illustration by Charlie Daniel, *Knoxville News Sentinel*.

Governor Bill Haslam's proposal to expand Medicaid not only would have saved lives, but would have saved tax dollars. Charlie Daniel agreed. Illustration by Charlie Daniel, *Knoxville News Sentinel.*

Many Republicans in the General Assembly repeatedly refused to co-operate with or follow the leadership of Republican governor Bill Haslam and accept the federal funds for Medicaid expansion to help working Tennesseans without health insurance.

This remained true even when the Tennessee Hospital Association, the Tennessee Hospital Alliance, and essentially all of Tennessee's hospitals agreed to provide the 10 percent match that would be required after three years to receive the 90 percent federal funding.

Numerous legislators have said to their constituents, and several have said directly to me, that they realize accepting the federal funding would be good for Tennessee and is the right thing to do. But they are fearful of someone running against them in a primary race and attacking them for accepting funds for "Obamacare."

They refuse to vote to accept the federal funding even from the Trump Administration. Even though Republican governors and legislatures lead many of the thirty-seven other states that currently accept the federal funds, Tennessee Republican legislators still refuse the funds. As a result, hospitals and Tennesseans die.

PART 3. RIGHTS

7
VOTERS' RIGHTS

Federal legislation protecting the right to vote was passed decades ago, but in recent years Tennesseans and other states have fought many battles over voting rights.

The bipartisan Tennessee Voter Confidence Act, passed without a single vote against it in 2008, made elections more secure by requiring "paper trail" verifications instead of relying solely on computerized systems. But when control of state and local elections shifted parties, those newly in control immediately sought to repeal that protection.

In 2011, legislation was passed to limit voting to those with only certain government-issued forms of identification. This new law excluded many forms of identification. Proponents alleged it would protect against election fraud, but in fact it disenfranchised many elderly, disabled, poor, rural, urban, and other citizens. The following two essays address those two issues.

TENNESSEE NEEDS PAPER TRAIL FOR EVERY VOTE (2011)

In 2008 the Tennessee legislature voted almost unanimously to make elections more secure, dependable, and trustworthy by requiring a verifiable paper trail for each vote. The step was long overdue—more than thirty states already have such security measures.

But three years later, secure elections in Tennessee remain at risk, and voters may never know if their votes are counted. If legislative Republicans' march toward passing a bill that would effectively repeal the *Voter Confidence Act* succeeds, it would be a devastating blow to democracy in Tennessee. The electronic voting machines used in ninety-three of our ninety-five counties are so vulnerable to fraud and thievery that they can steal your vote even before you cast your ballot.

The machines can be hacked at the factory, during transport, or the night before an election. They can be manipulated during and after an election with simple tools like paper clips and telephone cords. A New York University task force found that "paperless touch-screen voting machines," like "those presently used in parts of Tennessee, are the least secure voting system" in the entire country.

During early voting in 2008, there were reports in Decatur County, Tennessee, of so-called vote flipping. A *New York Times* editorial writers' blog noted that at least three voters complained "[electronic] voting machines registered their votes for Mr. [John] McCain as votes for Mr. [Barack] Obama."

In Arkansas, according to the *New York Times*, the mayor of Waldenburg discovered that these machines hadn't registered a single vote for him in a 2006 election—not even his own.

In Cleveland, Ohio, the newspaper reported, poll workers in 2007 had to use a paper trail to correct three-fourths of the ballots cast on machines just like ours.

From Texas to Florida, from Iowa to New Jersey, these machines have proved time and again that they are the equivalent of an open vault door to the most valuable treasure we have in a democracy: our vote.

There is no legitimate reason to continue to place our trust in electronic voting machines that have proved wholly unreliable. Yet today, we are closer than ever to repealing the bipartisan legislation enacted to safeguard our elections from fraud and malfunction.

Opponents of the *Voter Confidence Act* will say that local governments cannot bear the burden of implementing these more secure voting machines. Such arguments are a smoke screen.

Tennessee received $52 million from the federal government in 2003 for the sole purpose of making our elections more secure. Yet eight years later, $27 million remains in the fund, but our elections remain subject to fraud.

This should not be a partisan issue. The original bill was passed unanimously in the Senate and virtually unanimously in the House. But after Republicans took control of the General Assembly and the state's election commissions, suddenly the Republicans have reversed their position and now oppose *Voter Confidence Act* safeguards.

Several of our neighboring states, including North Carolina, Missouri, and Alabama, use optical scan machines with a verifiable paper trail.

This is not an urban-rural issue. States like New York and California with big cities have them. Rural states like West Virginia, Idaho, and the Dakotas have them.

Here in Tennessee, optical scan machines are used in a county as small as Pickett County and as large as Hamilton County, where officials told a state panel that they would highly recommend their machines.

We all have a stake in secure, legitimate elections. The strength of our political system lies in our citizens' trust that their votes count. Our current, easily manipulated, and too fallible voting machines endanger that trust.

We have waited too long to do the right thing. The *Voter Confidence Act* should not be repealed or delayed.

—"Tennessee Needs Paper Trail for Every Vote,"
Commercial Appeal, 5 May 2011.

Unfortunately, on partisan votes, the key protection in the Voter Confidence Act, the paper trail that lets voters be sure their votes count, was repealed. Pushed by the Republican Secretary of State and his election coordinator, all the Republican legislators and a few Democrats voted 71–25 in the House and 25–5–1 in the Senate for House Bill 386 that on June 3, 2011, became Public Chapter 301 of the Public Acts of 2011.

VOTER ID LAW WILL DISENFRANCHISE RURAL RESIDENTS (2011)

When my ninety-four-year-old mother was born, women were not allowed to vote. But then Tennessee ratified the Nineteenth Amendment, and for seven decades Mother has voted faithfully. This year, many of my Republican colleagues in the Legislature took away that right when they made it harder for her—and as many as 675,000 other Tennesseans—to continue to vote.

Ironically, all but seven legislators from the party that supposedly favors less government passed a law requiring my mother to obtain a "big-government"

When Republicans won control of both the Tennessee House and Senate in 2010, they immediately repealed the key protection of the Voter Confidence Act passed in the preceding session. Doing away with the "paper trail" requirement made it impossible for voters and election officials to be sure electronic machines were recording citizens' votes. Illustration by Charlie Daniel, *Knoxville News Sentinel*.

photo identity card in order to vote. When the law goes into effect with the March 2012 presidential primary, poll workers will no longer accept her voter registration card as sufficient proof of identity.

Mother has not driven in at least two decades, so she has no driver's license. But when she is pushed in her wheelchair to the polls, not one election worker will mistake her for another ninety-four-year-old trying to vote.

My mother is one of 675,337 Tennesseans age eighteen and older who, according to the Department of Safety, either have no driver's license or have a license that does not carry their photo. These citizens may be registered to vote, but unless they obtain a photo ID from a driver's license station or can produce another type of government-issued photo ID that the new law accepts (such as a military ID or a passport), they will not be allowed to vote.

One cannot get a government ID from the state Department of Safety without producing a "primary proof of identity," most commonly a birth certificate. Not surprisingly, my mother's 1916 birth certificate has been misplaced. So she and thousands of other registered voters like her will have to get new birth certificates, which is where the next problem arises.

To apply for a birth certificate, my mother must either travel to the state Department of Health's Office of Vital Records in Nashville, submit her request online, or telephone the office. Traveling nearly halfway across the state is not feasible for many elderly, disabled, mobility-challenged, poor, or employed Tennesseans. My mother and thousands of other Tennesseans are not computer literate, so they cannot order a birth certificate online.

I recently asked Annie Prescott, a Nashville attorney, to navigate the third option—a phone call to the Office of Vital Records. She spent the better part of an hour on the phone trying to speak to a live person. Over fifteen menu options offered by a series of recorded messages led to three busy signals and four hang ups. Finally, Prescott got a real person on the phone who instructed her to call a company that charges an additional $15 to process the $15 request, plus $5 to expedite service.

So the total cost of what is supposed to be a free state-issued photo ID card so far is $35, not counting the long-distance phone charges. And applicants still have to take the birth certificate to a driver's license testing station, where they may have to wait in line for hours.

Only forty-three of Tennessee's ninety-five counties have such centers. Eleven counties represented by seven Republicans who voted against this bill, including six from East Tennessee, don't have them. Some of the rural Tennesseans I represent will have to drive from their county through a second county and into a third to reach the closest driver's license center—a trip of forty to sixty miles each way. Taking a day off work and with gas averaging $3.58 a gallon, even at minimum wage the expense of travel and lost wages will cost people perhaps an additional $80 to $100 to exercise their constitutional right to vote.

The cost of this process—in many cases totaling $110 to $135 or more—is such a burden that for many it will amount to disenfranchisement.

Some claim this legislation is necessary to prevent voter fraud, citing a state Senate election in Memphis in 2005 in which votes were recorded from two deceased people. But the fact is that the culprits in that case were dishonest election workers, not voters. Photo ID cards would not solve that problem.

My family will do what's necessary so mother can continue to vote. But what about the other mothers and fathers, the blind, the hearing impaired, the disabled, the elderly, the poor, and the working people who already struggle to pay their bills, much less these new "poll taxes" of $100 or more to meet the requirements of the photo ID law?

I'm not opposed to voters having photo IDs, but I am opposed to taking away the right to vote through a bureaucratic system of poll taxes. People have died trying to register to vote. Now even those who are registered may still be denied the right to vote.

—"Voter ID Law Will Disenfranchise Rural Residents,"
Knoxville News Sentinel, 2 October 2011.
A similar essay was published in
the *Commercial Appeal* on September 25, 2011.

Since I wrote this op-ed in 2011, efforts to suppress the vote have continued not just in Tennessee but across the nation—and not just continued but seem to have grown in ferocity and mendacity. The following are but a few examples.

Before the 2016 election, almost a dozen election workers who collected and mailed ballots for elderly local voters were arrested in Texas for "unlawful assistance of a voter."[1]

In 2017 in Georgia, the Republican Secretary of State narrowly won a race for governor after he purged over three hundred thousand Georgia voters who had improperly been deemed "inactive."[2]

In 2018, operatives for a Republican congressional candidate in North Carolina were accused of illegally collecting and, in some cases, either tampering with or discarding thousands of absentee votes across the state to help secure his win.[3] The fraud was so drastic that the North Carolina Board of Elections ordered that a completely new special election be held.

1   Nicole Cobler, "Texas Prosecuted 15 Illegal Voting Cases, None Involving Impersonation," *Texas Tribune*, 22 August 2016, https://www.texastribune.org/2016/08/22/texas-prosecuted-15-illegal-voting-cases-none-invo/.

2   Alan Judd, "Georgia's Strict Laws Lead to Large Purge of Voters," *Atlanta Journal-Constitution*, 27 October 2018, https://www.ajc.com/news/state—regional-govt—politics/voter-purge-begs-question-what-the-matter-with-georgia/YAFvuk3Bu95kJIMaDiDFqJ/.

3   Leigh Ann Caldwell, Jeremia Kimelman, and Rich Gardella, "Absentee Ballots Will Be in the Spotlight at Hearing on North Carolina House Race," NBC News, 17 February 2019, https://www.nbcnews.com/politics/elections/absentee-ballots-will-be-spotlight-hearing-north-carolina-house-race-n972631.

In 2019, the US Supreme Court ruled that federal courts do not have the authority to stop partisan gerrymandering.[4] If you are a Republican voter in a district drawn to benefit Democrats in Maryland, or a Democratic voter in a district drawn to benefit Republicans in North Carolina, your vote may have been made meaningless, but the Supreme Court has ruled by five to four that the Constitution does not protect you.

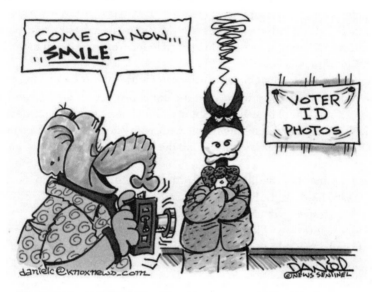

The legislature divided along party lines over new requirements denying voting by citizens without often hard to obtain government identification cards. In the author's district, obtaining such government identification cards required some citizens to leave their home county, drive through a second county, and go to a third county, where they still might not get the card required for voting even then. Illustration by Charlie Daniel, *Knoxville News Sentinel*.

---

4   Adam Liptak, "Supreme Court Green-Lights Gerrymandering and Blocks Census Citizenship Question," New York Times, 27 June 2019, https://www.nytimes.com/2019/06/27/us/politics/supreme-court-gerrymandering-census.html.

IT'S 50 YEARS SINCE CIVIL RIGHTS ACT OF '64 (2014)

Fifty years ago, when President Lyndon Johnson signed the Civil Rights Act of 1964, I was in elementary school and had no clue about the law that would drastically change daily life for African Americans. I surely had no idea how it would improve life for white Americans like me.

This historic legislation outlawed discrimination on the basis of race, color, religion, or national origin at "places of public accommodation." The movie theater I frequented had to discard its "coloreds only" entrance and the segregated balcony. Restaurants where we ate had to let African Americans out of the kitchens and into the dining areas. My future friends, like state Senator Reggie Tate of Memphis, were no longer excluded from admission to the Mid-South Fair six days a week.

The new law gave the US attorney general authority to seek redress when school boards deprived students "of the equal protection of the laws." Two years later, my school in Weakley County, Tennessee, was desegregated. And for the first time, I began to spend time daily with African American children. I had new friends in the classrooms, and the lessons went beyond reading and writing.

After signing the Civil Rights Act, President Johnson said to an aide, "We [Democrats] have lost the South for a generation." The president underestimated the political impact, which continues now *two* generations later.

In 1966, just two years later, the people of Tennessee for the first time popularly elected a Republican to the US Senate.

In 1968, in Memphis, the sanitation workers went on strike and Dr. Martin Luther King Jr. was struck down. In Nashville, the Republicans took control of the state House of Representatives for the first time since Reconstruction. Then in 1970, Tennessee elected a second Republican to the US Senate, throwing out Democratic senator Albert Gore Sr.

Despite the backlash, the Civil Rights Act changed customs and changed society. With those changes, what could not have been imagined in 1964 became reality in 2008: an African American was elected president.

Yet some Republicans responded to this historic progress with crude jokes and racist appeals to fellow bigots. In just one of many examples, a Tennessee Republican state legislative aide sent e-mails caricaturing President Barack Obama's official portrait as two cartoon eyes peering from a black background.

When I ran for Congress in 2010, racism was too easy to find. I can still see the angry face of the man at the duck supper who responded to my handshake with, "Lemme talk with you about your [N-word] president." And the scowling man at the rodeo who snarled, "I don't shake hands with darkies or Democrats—and they're often the same."

Thankfully, most Republicans are not racists. But while most Republicans would never discriminate, degrade, or demean, their leaders' legislative actions still repress voters and reverse progress.

All over the country, Republicans are pushing new impediments to discourage and decrease voting by minorities and low-income citizens. While Republicans say they oppose big and oppressive government, they rammed through Tennessee's voter ID law, now notorious as one of the nation's most burdensome. Only certain government-issued photo ID cards now are acceptable at the polls, after Republicans outlawed using a Social Security card or even photo ID cards from the Memphis public library or the University of Memphis. Those without a driver's license—nationally, 25 percent of African Americans—now must go to a driver's license station to obtain a photo ID card if they wish to vote, but fewer than half of Tennessee's counties even have such a station.

Republicans claim these laws fight voter fraud, but instances of persons trying to vote while using someone else's identity are almost nonexistent. And in a recent study researchers at the University of Southern California showed strong evidence that "discriminatory intent underlies legislative support for [these new] voter identification laws."

The first book of the Bible teaches, "So God created humankind in his own image, in the image of God he created them." God's image does not have a color, but it does have a creed. The Apostle Paul put it this way in Galatians 3: "There is neither Jew nor Greek, there is neither slave nor free, there is neither male nor female, for you are all one in Christ Jesus."

Our American ideals long have taught that we are one. The Great Seal of the United States proclaims "E pluribus unum"—from many, one.

But it was just fifty years ago today that statesmen and idealists and people of a deep faith in Almighty God and in America together created the Civil Rights Act of 1964. Let us celebrate their good work for justice and freedom. And let us carry on their good work, so all God's children can live in peace and love in truth.

—"It's 50 Years since Civil Rights Act of '64,"
Commercial Appeal, 2 July 2014.
Similar essays were published in *TNReport* and in
Chattanooga Times Free Press on July 3, 2014.

Battles over voting rights continue today.

In 2013, the Supreme Court struck down the heart of the Voting Rights Act of 1965, which required certain states to have federal approval before changing their voting laws.[5]

These states, mostly Southern states with a history of discouraging minorities from voting, have been able to pursue without oversight or restriction legislation and practices that disproportionately discriminate against and disenfranchise minority voters.

In 2013, Charlie Daniel weighed in on the Supreme Court decision striking down a central protection of the Voting Rights Act that was passed the year after the Civil Rights Act the author honored in the previous essay. Illustration by Charlie Daniel, *Knoxville News Sentinel.*

5   Adam Liptak, "Supreme Court Invalidates Key Part of Voting Rights Act," *New York Times,* 25 June 2013, https://www.nytimes.com/2013/06/26/us/supreme-court-ruling.html.

8
WOMEN'S RIGHTS

Passionate citizens and strong organizations pushed Senate Joint Resolution 127 throughout multiple General Assemblies. The legislation was designed to overturn the Tennessee Supreme Court decision in *Planned Parenthood of Middle Tennessee, et al. v. Don Sundquist, Governor of the State of Tennessee, et al.* that in 2000 held "a woman's right to terminate her pregnancy is a vital part of the right to privacy guaranteed by the Tennessee Constitution." After approval by the General Assembly in 2011, SJR 127 went before the people in 2014 as Amendment One.

This essay deals with when women's lives are endangered by pregnancy. The second essay addresses when women are impregnated by rapists. The third essay seeks to rebut an effective but misleading argument by proponents of Amendment One.[1]

---

1   The Constitution of Tennessee was amended to include the following: "Nothing in this Constitution secures or protects a right to abortion or requires the funding of an abortion. The people retain the right through their elected state representatives and state senators to enact, amend, or repeal statutes regarding abortion, including, but not limited to, circumstances of pregnancy resulting from rape or incest or when necessary to save the life of the mother." Originally a resolution sponsored by Senator Diane Black and Senator Mae Beavers, this amendment passed the Tennessee General Assembly and was placed on the ballot in the 2014 election. Tennessee voters narrowly approved the amendment.

These op-eds were written to protect rape victims and women facing life-threatening pregnancies and to allow these victims, not government, to make their own difficult decisions.

A WOMAN'S RIGHT TO SAVE HER LIFE (2014)

This year, Tennesseans will vote on whether to take personal decisions away from women and their doctors and give the power to the politicians. I'm reminded of one such personal decision involving a woman, a doctor, and me.

While carrying twins during our first pregnancy, my wife had complications. Nancy and I went to a Nashville hospital for a high-resolution ultrasound. The specialist said he'd seen this particular complication sixteen times. In fifteen of those cases, both twins had died. In the other case, one twin survived.

Thirty-two babies. Thirty-one dead.

The doctor said our twins were not going to live. He recommended an abortion.

"How sure are you, doctor?" I asked.

The doctor said he was pretty sure.

"Like 90, 95, 98 percent certain?"

He replied, "Yes."

The doctor again recommended abortion.

Nancy was in tears. I tried to choke back tears. I finally managed to get out the questions pounding inside my head: "Is Nancy's life in danger? Is the abortion needed to save her life?"

In the instant before the doctor replied, Nancy and I came to opposite conclusions. She was willing to lose her life for the babies. I was not willing to lose her. Fortunately, Nancy was in no more danger than with any other high-risk pregnancy. And, by God's grace, we found another physician who saved our babies—they are now twenty-three!

While Nancy and I felt differently about what we should have done if her life had been in grave danger, we both agree that politicians should not have decided for us. Instead, we believe such a decision should be made by the couple, with the help of the best physicians and the most faithful pastors, with the best of medical science and with the most fervent of prayers.

Many advocates of Amendment One, however, believe the decision whether to save a woman's life shouldn't be made with the help of Almighty God but instead should be taken away by Almighty Government.

When I was in the Tennessee legislature, the sister of one of our interns was diagnosed with cancer. She had just gotten pregnant. To increase her chances of survival, the doctor recommended ending the pregnancy. Should politicians take away from that young woman and her husband the right to choose life, her life?

A legislator's sister went into labor. Her struggles grew more and more severe; the dangers to her life increased and became serious. The doctor asked her husband's permission to take the baby's life, if necessary, to save the mother. Would we tell that husband and doctor they could not save her life?

Ralph Duncan is a pastor who once served in the Tennessee House of Representatives. This man of God is ardently anti-abortion. Yet he and his wife found themselves in a tragic situation, in which her life was imperiled and there were no good options. The doctor told the pastor he could lose his baby or he could lose his baby and his wife. But the baby would not survive.

Pastor Duncan and his wife chose the less awful option and saved her life. Would we let politicians make Ralph Duncan into a criminal or force this pastor's wife to die?

This year Tennesseans will vote on Amendment One, a deceptively worded and flawed constitutional amendment that would let politicians take these decisions away from women and their doctors.

Amendment One would eliminate from our constitution any protection for the life of the mother. The language could not be broader: "Nothing in this Constitution secures or protects a right to abortion." Not even to save her life.

When this issue came before the General Assembly, I was in the Senate. I offered an amendment to preserve a constitutional "life of the mother" exception, but Tea Party Republicans unanimously rejected it.

Why would they do so? Because they wished to make abortion illegal in every situation and circumstance? Because they believed that it is simply God's will that these women die in pregnancy or childbirth?

Amendment One would let politicians take the power of life and death away from women and their doctors, leaving women with no state constitutional protection even to save their own lives.

Imagine watching your wife or sister or mother die needlessly while you sit there, helpless, powerless, because Tea Party Republicans decided to sacrifice her on the altar of their ideology.

Imagine if the woman about to die was someone you love.

Or was you.

Tennessee Senator Charlotte Burks is the widow of a state senator. Her late husband, Senator Tommy Burks, was murdered by his political opponent. She succeeded her husband to the same office.

Senator Burks continued to represent the views and values she and her late husband share with her district. Among those values is a commitment to protect the unborn. She is unashamedly pro-life.

When this legislation was on the floor of the Tennessee Senate, which would have begun the process of amending our state constitution to remove any state constitutional right to an abortion, Senator Burks supported the legislation. She wanted, however, to let women whose lives were truly endangered by pregnancy be able to decide whether they could save their own lives.

When the pro-life Senator Burks sponsored an amendment to protect these girls and women—and also to constitutionally ban partial-birth abortion—some attacked her politically. Flyers were handed out in her district. And then came the death threat.

An anonymous male called Senator Burks's office and snarled, "I'm going to kill the baby killer!"

Can you imagine such a threat against a woman whose husband had been murdered by a political opponent a few short years earlier? Can you imagine how she and her daughters felt?

But in the face of numerous political threats and even this death threat, Senator Burks refused to bow. In fact, any chance this devout and courageous Christian would change her mind ended with that threat to her life.

Women whose lives are endangered should have the right to risk their lives— or to save them. Amendment One would take the right away.

—"A Woman's Right to Save Her Life,"
Commercial Appeal, 5 October 2014.

AMENDMENT ONE LEAVES NO EXCEPTIONS FOR VICTIMS OF RAPE (2014)

A Baptist pastor called my law office. He needed legal counsel about a girl in his church. Her father had molested the girl since she was nine. Finally, when she was fourteen, she told friends at school. Why? Because she was pregnant with her father's child.

Ultimately, that "father" went to prison, and that child had an abortion. The father should have gone to prison. Whether the child should have had an abortion, I do not claim to know. It was not my decision to make. Nor was it a decision for politicians. The decision was made by the victim and her mother with the compassionate counsel of her doctor and pastor.

I do not trust politicians to have all the answers. Especially not in horrible situations involving rape or incest. I believe that compassionate, caring, faithful adults, like that loving mother and pastor and doctor, ought to make or help make these difficult decisions.

My wife hears the criminal injury claims of hundreds of victims, including rape victims, victims as young as seven. Numerous young teens. She also hears cases of adult rape victims.

She's heard many cases where young women were given a date-rape drug, then assaulted. She's heard countless cases where young women were raped at knifepoint and gunpoint and by brutal force. When some of these girls and women are impregnated by their rapists, should we also force our government upon them and require them to bear the rapists' children?

Rape of a child under thirteen is a Class A felony, the most serious classification for the most serious crime. It is punishable by up to sixty years in prison. Yet, would we have the same government that deems child rape the most heinous of crimes also tell a twelve-year-old victim that she must continue to be tortured by the rapist for nine more months? Would we tell the child, no matter how traumatized or devastated, that she must bear that child, then either raise the rapist's child or abandon it?

I was a state senator when Amendment One was before the legislature. During that controversy, two friends told me their daughters were raped and had conceived. These mothers asked me to try to protect victims like their daughters.

Amendment One is a flawed and dangerous proposal. If approved, politicians would pass more restrictions making ending pregnancies difficult or impossible, even in cases of rape and incest.

When this proposed Amendment One was in the Senate, I offered amendments to let victims of rape and incest and women whose lives are endangered decide. Every Republican voted against the amendments, and the amendments failed. So, Amendment One would leave no state constitutional protection for these victims.

In tragic circumstances, families deserve to make their own difficult, private decisions, without government interference.

Women and their doctors, not politicians, know what's best for women. As a young woman who is pro-life but anti-Amendment One told me last week, "I'm against all abortions, but I ought not try to decide for everyone else." She believes it is better that each woman makes her own private decision, in consultation with her family, doctor, and faith.

If you want politicians to make these decisions even in cases of child rape and incest, then vote yes for Amendment One.

But if you agree that we should not let politicians require women and girls whose lives already are devastated to bear rapists' children, then vote no on Amendment One.

—"Amendment 1 Leaves No Exceptions for Victims of Rape,"
Chattanooga Times Free Press, 6 October 2014.

AMENDMENT ONE WOULD DESTROY, NOT "NEUTRALIZE" RIGHTS (2014)

During early voting or on November 4, you will vote on a state constitutional amendment to strip a woman of her right to make a terribly difficult, personal decision. Instead of letting a woman decide with her faith, her family, and her doctor, Amendment One would let politicians restrict and potentially prohibit all abortions with no exceptions for rape or incest or even to save a woman's life.

Tea Party Republicans say they want to "neutralize" the state constitution on abortion. But what if politicians wanted to "neutralize" our First Amendment right to free speech, leaving it to politicians to decide whether we citizens can criticize the government?

Or would we want politicians to "neutralize" the First Amendment's free exercise of religion clause, so they can decide how or whether we can worship God?

What if politicians were to "neutralize" the Second Amendment to the US Constitution, leaving it up to politicians to decide if they want to abolish our right to bear arms?

Tennessee Amendment One would not merely "neutralize" the state constitution, but instead would destroy every woman's right to decide whether to end a pregnancy, regardless of circumstance.

Amendment One means simply this: politicians can help you if they will or harm you if they won't. Amendment One is an attempt by politicians to deny Tennessee women, even victims of rape or incest or life-threatening illness, the right to make their own personal, private decisions. These decisions are best left to women and their doctors—not politicians.

But the state senate sponsor of Amendment One admitted that, if Amendment One passes, and the US Supreme Court decision in *Roe v. Wade* is overturned, then the law in Tennessee would be whatever as few as 50 of 99 representatives and 17 of 33 senators decide.

When women's lives are endangered or they are the victims of rape or incest, we ought not leave the victims' fates to current politicians or unknown future legislators. Rather, the cautious, conservative, constitutional approach is to protect victims with Tennessee's constitution, not imperil them with this overly broad provision that would strip victims of any state constitutional protection.

When a recent Vanderbilt University poll asked if Tennesseans would favor giving state legislators more power to regulate abortions, citizens by a 3–1 margin said, "No." If Tennesseans are not misled about Amendment One, women can be protected, and women can win.

If you think politicians should decide for you or your daughter, even in cases of rape and incest, or when a woman's life is in endangered by pregnancy, then vote for this amendment. But if you agree that government should not further victimize the victims of rape or incest or life-threatening illness, then please protect our constitutional rights and vote against Amendment One.

—"Amendment 1 Would Destroy, Not 'Neutralize' Rights,"
The Tennessean, 8 October 2014.

> To amend Tennessee's Constitution requires that a majority of those voting in the race for Governor approve any constitutional amendment on the ballot at the same time. In 2014, Amendment One was narrowly approved by the voters of Tennessee. Those voting for Amendment One were 729,163, and those voting against it were 657,192, or 52.60 percent to 47.40 percent.[2]
>
> Today, Tennesseans have no state constitutional protections when it comes to abortion. If the US Supreme Court strikes down *Roe v. Wade*, as it appears recent appointees to the Court may well provide the votes to do, then nothing in Tennessee's Constitution will protect even women whose lives are endangered. Their rights and their protections will be whatever "fifty and seventeen" in the Tennessee House and Senate decide.[3]

---

2   A total of 1,353,728 voted for Governor. But under Tennessee's Constitution, this meant that 676,865 votes in favor of Amendment One were required, which meant the Amendment actually only passed by about 50,000 votes.

3   As a number of states have moved to pass laws that would make abortion illegal with no exceptions, an August 13, 2019, Public Religion Research Institute survey of over forty thousand Americans in all fifty states finds only 15 percent of Americans overall say abortion should be illegal in all cases. See https://www.prri.org/research/legal-in-most-cases-the-impact-of-the-abortion-debate-in-2019-america/. Notably, there is no state in which more than one-quarter of residents support making abortion services completely illegal.

In 2014, churches and communities were divided over a state constitutional amendment dealing with abortion. The vote was historically close—had 36,000 out of 1,380,000 votes gone against it instead of for it, Amendment One would not have passed. Illustration by Charlie Daniel, *Knoxville News Sentinel*.

9
CRIME VICTIMS' RIGHTS

Before 1998, the Tennessee Constitution provided twenty-seven rights for those accused and convicted of crimes but literally no rights for crime victims. I sponsored and with others pushed to amend the state Constitution to include the Crime Victims' Bill of Rights.

The next essay was published while the legislation was being considered in the General Assembly. The second essay was written when the amendment had been placed on the ballot and was being considered by Tennessee's voters.

CRIME VICTIMS DESERVE THE RIGHT TO BE HEARD (1996)

On a pretty September day in the peaceful West Tennessee town of Greenfield, Charlotte Stout's eight-year-old daughter rode her bicycle in a church parking lot.

A man drove up and tricked her into his car. He took Charlotte Stout's little Carey to a nearby farm. There, he brutally raped her. Then he murdered her.

That was sixteen years ago.

Charlotte Stout, whom I represent in the legislature, told our House Judiciary Committee:

Since the trial, I have not been contacted one time to notify me of hearings, appeals, or anything regarding the man who killed my daughter. I
have been contacted by newspaper and TV reporters for my comments
on yet another event in his appeals process, of which I was totally unaware
or didn't understand. . . .

It's beyond belief that a person who commits a crime is required to
be read his constitutional rights, and yet the victims and their families
are left to figure it out on their own.

Why are crime victims, unlike criminals, not read their constitutional rights?
Because they have none.

Not one.

Tennessee's Constitution provides twenty-seven rights for those accused
and convicted of crimes but no rights for their victims.

No wonder Charlotte Stout complains, "It seems our whole criminal justice
system is upside down!"

Two hundred years ago, when the entire state was rural, everyone knew
everyone else, and prosecutors often were hired by the victims. Crime victims
were heard. Victims needed no constitutional rights to protect them.

Today, Charlotte Stout's experience is common.

Such experiences are not limited to those suffering during years of appeals.
Recently, I went to court with a crime victim. The busy prosecutor told me,
"The deal's already done." The lawyer for the criminal who brutally beat my
client and her daughter had bargained to have the aggravated assault charge
reduced and another assault charge dismissed altogether.

While I pleaded in the hallway, the "deal" was presented in the courtroom.
We walked in just in time to raise a fuss as the man who had beaten my client
beyond recognition was about to walk out.

Eventually, after I complained and pleaded, the judge ordered the criminal
to pay my client's hospital bills. And the charge for beating my client's young
daughter was not dismissed.

But what about the thousands of victims without lawyers?

For five years, Tennessee has had a statute that was supposed to protect
victims. It has failed. Terribly.

Tennessee now can do what twenty other states already have done: really
protect crime victims by placing their rights in our constitution.

House Joint Resolution 14, which the House passed and now is in the Senate, would let Tennesseans vote to amend our constitution to create the Crime Victims' Bill of Rights.

Those rights in the criminal justice process would be:

1. The right to confer with the prosecution.
2. The right to be free from intimidation, harassment, and abuse.
3. The right to attend proceedings the defendant has the right to attend.
4. The right to be heard, when relevant, at critical stages.
5. The right to be informed of proceedings, and of the release, transfer, or escape of the accused or convicted person.
6. The right to a speedy trial or disposition and a prompt and final conclusion of the case.
7. The right to restitution from the offender.
8. The right to be informed of each of these rights.

I know there is reluctance to amend our constitution. I myself initially was reluctant to do so.

The other sponsors and I greatly respect our constitution. The House Judiciary Committee moved deliberately over many weeks to consider carefully what should be done.

We know some remain opposed. The American Civil Liberties Union argues, "It's dangerous to mess with the Constitution."

But what about the danger to my client and her daughter who were savagely beaten and told, "The deal's already done"?

What about the danger to Charlotte Stout and other victims with no constitutional right to know when criminals who killed and raped are going to be released?

If our national constitution had not been amended, we would not have the Bill of Rights in the first ten amendments. Slavery would not have been outlawed by the Thirteenth Amendment. And there would be no due process and equal protection rights under the Fourteenth Amendment.

As we celebrate the seventy-fifth anniversary of Tennessee approving the Nineteenth Amendment giving women the right to vote, we ought not be unduly fearful of also giving crime victims the right to be heard.

The Crime Victims' Bill of Rights can change our Constitution to keep pace with the times, these very dangerous times.

—"Crime Victims Deserve the Right to Be Heard,"
Jackson Sun, 1996.

In 1996, forty representatives joined me in sponsoring House Joint Resolution 14.[1]

It was approved in the Tennessee House of Representatives by a vote of 93 to 0. The bill was then sponsored in the Senate by my friend, the late Senator Tommy Burks, and the Tennessee Senate concurred by a vote of 28 to 4.

Tennessee's Constitution requires, however, that constitutional amendments must be approved by two different general assemblies, the second time by two-thirds of each house.

By 1998, I was serving in the Senate. Working with Senator Burks again, the Senate overwhelmingly passed Senate Joint Resolution 2. The legislation then passed the House by a vote of 98 to 0.[2]

The proposed constitutional amendment then went before the people for their consideration. At that time, the following op-ed was published. That was shortly after Senator Tommy Burks himself was murdered.

BALANCING THE SCALES OF JUSTICE (1998)

Tennessee voters will decide on Tuesday whether our state's constitution will have a bill of rights for crime victims. That includes the right to confer with the prosecution, the right to be present in court whenever the defendant has a right to be present, the right to a speedy trial, and the right to notice of hearings on releasing convicted criminals.

State Senator Tommy Burks, who was murdered last month, worked with us, other lawmakers, and victims for four years to put the Crime Victims' Bill of Rights on the ballot. His widow and children, and all other crime victims, deserve the protection of Tennessee's Constitution.

Criminals and criminal suspects have twenty-seven rights enumerated in our Constitution. Crime victims have none.

Two centuries ago, when neighbors and kin helped prosecute criminals, victims needed no constitutional protection by government. But that day is long gone, and this imbalance should be redressed. Fairness requires that the victims of constitutionally protected criminals should have similar protection.

---

1   For information related to HJR 14, see "HJR0014," Legislation, Tennessee General Assembly, http://wapp.capitol.tn.gov/apps/BillInfo/Default.aspx?BillNumber=HJR0014&GA=99.

2   "SJR0002," Legislation, Tennessee General Assembly, http://wapp.capitol.tn.gov/apps/BillInfo/default.aspx?BillNumber=SJR0002&GA=100.

Changing the Constitution is serious business. Only reluctantly and slowly did we come to believe that was the right course. We concluded that laws aimed at protecting victims' rights, which have been on the books for a decade, have failed.

From one end of the state to the other, no one—not victims, judges, prosecutors, or even defense attorneys—maintains that statutory rights are observed as they should be. And other rights that victims need, including a right to a speedy trial, have been defeated.

Our decision to attempt to change the Constitution came after we listened to victims failed by the criminal justice system. The leaders on this issue have been mostly women—people such as Charlotte Stout from Weakley County.

Almost two decades ago, Charlotte Stout's eight-year-old daughter was riding her bicycle when a demented, dangerous man tricked the little girl into a car. He brutally raped and murdered her.

As related in the previous essay in more detail, Charlotte Stout came to the General Assembly and testified about that case, which today continues in endless appeals and proceedings. Her problems emerged after the trial; local prosecutors have not handled the appeals. But problems also arise at the trial court level.

The local system failed Debi and Roger Richardson of West Tennessee, whose young son was murdered by a gang firing a high-powered rifle and a sawed-off shotgun. The police immediately apprehended the killers, but three years later trials and plea bargains still were not concluded.

The parents suffered not only the loss of their son but also victimization by a criminal justice system that moved too slowly and added rather than alleviated pain.

When one of the cases finally came to trial, the killer had a right to be in the courtroom. But he could keep the victim's own mother, who was going to testify, out of that courtroom.

Rebecca Easley's sister Deborah Groseclose was brutally murdered in Memphis twenty-one years ago. In a few months, those convicted of the murder will be tried again.

Deborah Groseclose left behind two small children, one of whom now has her own child. Deborah's grandparents, father, and brother did not survive the appeals. Rebecca Easley wonders if she will.

The Crime Victims' Bill of Rights will give Charlotte Stout, Debi and Roger Richardson, Rebecca Easley, Senator Burks's family, and other victims the constitutional rights that can protect them from further victimization by criminals. It also can protect them from insensitivity, callousness, or malfeasance by government.

The ballot proposal will not diminish any of the state constitutional rights guaranteed an accused citizen or a convicted criminal. But it will give crime victims constitutional rights for the first time. Some of those rights are not now part of state law.

The amendment will make Tennessee the 30th state to protect crime victims with constitutional rights. Among the groups that endorse the proposal are the Tennessee Sheriffs' Association, the Tennessee Association of Chiefs of Police, the Tennessee District Attorneys General Conference, the American Association of Retired Persons, Mothers Against Drunk Driving, the National Victims' Center, and crime victims' organizations across our state.

These groups recognize what so many crime victims know: it is time to balance the scales of justice.

—Co-authored with Representative Jere Hargrove.
"Balancing the Scales of Justice," *Commercial Appeal*, 1 November 1998.

Two crime victims, a mother whose child was murdered and a woman whose sister suffered the same fate, here advocated for the Crime Victims' Bill of Rights. The author sponsored that constitutional amendment with Senator Tommy Burks before he was murdered. His widow, Charlotte Burks, ran for his Senate seat, won, and helped push the amendment into law. Photo property of author.

On November 3, 1998, the citizens of Tennessee voted to approve the constitutional amendment creating the Crime Victims' Bill of Rights. The vote was 680,712 to 85,565. By a margin of 88.8 percent to 11.2 percent it became part of our Constitution.[3]

The exact language now in Tennessee's Constitution is found in Article One at Section 35:

> To preserve and protect the rights of victims of crime to justice and due process, victims shall be entitled to the following basic rights:
> 1. The right to confer with the prosecution.
> 2. The right to be free from intimidation, harassment and abuse throughout the criminal justice system.
> 3. The right to be present at all proceedings where the defendant has the right to be present.
> 4. The right to be heard, when relevant, at all critical stages of the criminal justice process as defined by the General Assembly.
> 5. The right to be informed of all proceedings, and of the release, transfer or escape of the accused or convicted person.
> 6. The right to a speedy trial or disposition and a prompt and final conclusion of the case after the conviction or sentence.
> 7. The right to restitution from the offender.
> 8. The right to be informed of each of the rights established for victims.

The General Assembly has the authority to enact substantive and procedural laws to define, implement, preserve and protect the rights guaranteed to victims by this section.

---

3   "Tennessee Victims' Bill of Rights, Amendment 2 (1998)," Ballotpedia, https://ballotpedia .org/tennessee_victims%27_bill_of_rights,_amendment_2_(1998).

PART 4. EDUCATION

10
EDUCATION

Political leadership has been crucial to the improvement of Tennessee's schools.

In 1983, Governor Alexander implemented his Better Schools program, which standardized basic skills for all students and increased math, science, and computer education. A portion of this plan, known as Master Teachers, or Career Ladder, called for income supplements for the state's top teachers, and an amended version of the bill passed.

Governor McWherter increased appropriations for K–12 public education, and in 1992 his Twenty-First Century Schools program upgraded facilities, lowered teacher–student ratios, and addressed inequities of public education funding between rural and urban counties.

Governor Sundquist fought for education funding for Tennessee to compete with our Southern neighbors.

Governor Bredesen led in the enactment of a number of measures aimed at improving education, including raising teachers' pay above the Southeast average, expanding Tennessee's prekindergarten initiative to include a statewide program for four-year-olds, and increasing funding for education.

The author's sons (left to right) Ben, Rick, and John teach their dad in their new school library. Photo: Dean Dixon.

The author visits students in the computer lab at his hometown elementary school. Photo: Dean Dixon.

Governor Haslam's signature education was the implementation of the Tennessee Promise program guaranteeing that Tennessee high school graduates can attend an in-state community or technical college tuition-free. He also initiated Tennessee Reconnect, which helps adults return to colleges to finish degrees or earn new ones.

Tennessee has faced many challenges in making sure all of our children can receive a quality public education. When Japan's economy was roaring and its highly intelligent citizens were rightfully admired, I reflected on Tennessee's challenges by taking insights from Japan's educational system. The following essay reflects on what we can learn from Japan to help schools here.

After that are two essays addressing Governor Bill Lee's 2019 voucher legislation to give public tax dollars to private schools.

WHERE EDUCATION IS A PRIORITY AND WHERE IT IS NOT (2002)

Last summer, I invested weeks—but no tax dollars—studying Japan's educational system for lessons we might apply here.

In Tokyo, our twins played with another fifth grader. Kyo also attends a public school seven hours each weekday. Unlike John and Rick, however, three days each week, Kyo is tutored for three more hours. Some estimate half of Japan's children receive such "cram schooling."

Kyo also attends school every other Saturday. His summer vacation is half as long as John and Rick's—just six weeks—during which Kyo has private instruction and completes public school assignments. Kyo's fifth grade includes the equivalent of eighteen weeks more instruction than John and Rick's. At that rate, when our sons complete the twelfth grade, Kyo will have had the equivalent of eighteen grades.

Even without tutoring, Kyo's poorer classmates go to school about ten more weeks a year than Tennessee children.

Is it any wonder that Japanese children rank far ahead of our own in math and science?

Japan, destroyed by war, with half our population, a fraction of our land, and almost none of our natural resources, built itself into an economic power second only to the United States. How? Through hard work and especially by investing in education.

An economic recession has hindered Japan for years, and its government struggles. But the Japanese are zealously committed to educating their children and to excelling in economic competition. When two hundred Japanese companies in Tennessee decide to build new plants, what will we say to attract those or other Japanese companies?

That two-thirds of Tennessee students are not proficient readers and we are the only Southeastern state without a state-funded reading initiative?

That we rank forty-sixth in the percentage of citizens with high school diplomas? Or that we fell further behind in 2000 as our public high school graduation rate ranked fiftieth?

Our former US Senator, Howard Baker, is now ambassador to Japan. He does not want to tell Japanese business leaders that our K–12 education investing on a per capita basis ranks fiftieth and only three dollars a person ahead of fifty-first Arkansas. The National Center for Public Policy and Higher Education grades us a D-minus for participation in higher education. Only one state ranks lower. And things are getting worse.

Our higher education "growth" in state appropriations from 1988 to 2000, adjusted for inflation and enrollment, is minus 3.1 percent. From 1995 to 2000, general operating appropriations in inflation-adjusted dollars at our public four-year universities fell $1,303 per student. Not one of the fifteen other states in the Southern Regional Education Board (SREB) did worse.

Among public four-year institutions in the sixteen SREB states: Tennessee ranks eleventh in full professor pay, fourteenth for associate and assistant professors, and fifteenth for instructors.

For two-year institutions, we rank second from the bottom in paying full professors, next to last for associate and assistant professors, and dead last for instructors.

Is it any wonder we are losing our finest faculty? To replace them, we recruit whoever is left after virtually every other state gets its pick.

What if the Vols or Vandy could award athletic scholarships only after every other SEC university signed whom they wanted? What if the Titans drafted only after every other NFL team?

In per capita state and local government expenditures for kindergarten through higher education, Tennessee ranks dead last. That's right: fifty-first of the fifty states and DC.

What investors from Japan or any country or state will want to come here, when every other state invests more in educating its workforce? And how many of our best and brightest young people, too many of whom are going out of state for college, will return to invest their lives in Tennessee?

Apart from the global war on terrorism, there is another war today. It is an economic competition that will decide who will lead and who will follow, who will prosper and who will suffer, who will be the thinkers and doers and who will be paid less because they are less skilled and less educated. This economic world war is taking place in a new, different Information Age. The world is moving into this age as surely as we moved from an Agricultural Age to an Industrial Age. And in this new age, Tennessee risks losing the war.

No state has better people than Tennessee. But our fine people are threatened by decreasing prospects for the future if we do not make the needed investments in education.

Our children can compete with anybody's, if given the opportunities they need. But to succeed, they need us to do right by them.

Whatever Japan's shortcomings, the Japanese recognize that educating their citizens is crucial to their future. Will we?

—"Where Education Is a Priority and Where It Is Not,"
The Tennessean, 24 March 2002.
A similar essay was published in the *Commercial Appeal* on October 7, 2001.

Improving Tennessee public schools is an issue for every General Assembly, with tune-ups and overhauls virtually every year. Illustration by Charlie Daniel, *Knoxville News Sentinel.*

Tennessee's teachers and students often vastly outperform legislators and governors, whose failures in funding education Charlie Daniel did not overlook. Illustration by Charlie Daniel, *Knoxville News Sentinel.*

EDUCATION SAVINGS ACCOUNTS ARE JUST ANOTHER VOUCHER SCHEME RIPE FOR ABUSE (2019)

Would you like your tax dollars being used to buy Mercedes Benz cars and abortions? Would you like your taxes going up? Or your public schools going down? Or both?

For a decade, Tennessee legislators have repeatedly rejected radical school voucher plans to give away public dollars to private schools. Now billionaire-funded out-of-state interest groups have rebranded school vouchers as "education savings accounts." ESAs are a way to put lipstick on a pig.

ESAs are debit cards loaded with tax dollars intended to pay for private or home schooling or other educational services.

They are vouchers on steroids—less accountability, more fraud, and an even greater drain on our public schools.

Abuse of ESAs Abounds throughout the Nation

Luxury cars and high-definition TVs are just two examples of what vouchers and ESAs have purchased. In 2015, an Arizona woman was indicted for using an ESA to pay for an abortion.

The *Orlando Sentinel's* investigation of Florida's ESA and voucher programs found enough spending scandals to publish an entire series of stories called "Schools without Rules."

ESA advocates always promise strict accountability. But audits of Arizona's ESA program documented hundreds of thousands of dollars in fraud even after adopting stricter accountability laws.

If you want to maximize the abuse of tax dollars, hand out ESA debit cards and then try to police hundreds of thousands of transactions by thousands of recipients. If you want to undermine education, give addicted parents thousands of tax dollars to home school or virtual school so parents can game the system to support their drug habits and fuel the opioid crisis.

Louisiana, Ohio, and Wisconsin all started with single-city "pilot programs" and then went statewide. In Florida, annual spending on vouchers and ESAs has grown by 1,832 percent, from $50 million to nearly $1 billion. Arizona's spending has grown by 1,700 percent. Wisconsin started with $700,000 and is now over $300 million a year—a staggering growth of over 43,000 percent.

Studies in Indiana, Ohio, and Louisiana all documented vouchers' negative impacts on children. A Louisiana study found voucher students' math scores dropped twenty-four points. Even a study funded by a pro-voucher foundation found negative effects on Ohio student performance.

ESAs Amount to "Welfare for the Wealthy"

ESAs and vouchers often are welfare for the wealthy. In Wisconsin, three-quarters of vouchers go to students already attending private schools.

Most Indiana students using vouchers have never enrolled in a public school.

ESAs require tax dollars to support both private- and public-school systems, so they take taxes up or schools down. Or both. If just a small percentage of Tennessee public school students took ESAs, replacing lost public-school funding could send property taxes soaring.

A recent Stanford University study found Tennessee's schools are the nation's fastest improving. Why would we risk that progress for a program that has left other states falling behind?

ESAs are proven failures. They expand and drain ever more money from public schools. And they are an entitlement—educational welfare used too often by those who don't need our tax dollars and the dishonest who abuse them. Tennessee legislators should reject ESAs.

—Co-Authored with Rick Herron.
"Education Savings Accounts Are Just Another Voucher Scheme Ripe for Abuse,"
The Tennessean, 11 March 2019.

THE TENNESSEE EDUCATION SAVINGS ACCOUNT BILL FAILS THE MATH TEST (2019)

Governor Bill Lee has proposed legislation that would create a $125 million a year voucher entitlement program. Governor Lee says his $7,300 per child Education Savings Account (ESA) bill would help Tennessee's poorest children in our worst-performing schools.

We applaud the governor's emphasis on education, and we believe in his good intentions. But unfortunately, others have drafted a bill that would let millionaires and even billionaires qualify for this voucher entitlement, while the poorest children are left behind.

The voucher math doesn't add up. The $7,300 voucher would leave poor kids far short on cash for quality private schools' tuition and fees, which can be two or three or even four times as much.

The Mega-rich Could Qualify for Vouchers

Even if poor kids could find a less expensive private school, few would have transportation to private school neighborhoods. Poor kids in single-parent or no-parent homes, who often don't have cars, would remain figuratively and literally stranded.

One respected voucher proponent characterizes this bill as a "windfall" for public schools. But if he had gotten $35,000 per year in vouchers for his five home- and private-schooled children for K–12, he'd have received almost a half million of your tax dollars.

Another vigorous voucher proponent also keeps his children out of public schools. Vouchers for seven children from kindergarten through high school could have paid him nearly $700,000. And if this bill passes, you may yet pay him—and many others like him—hundreds of thousands.

Even wealthy families could receive ESA vouchers. The current Senate bill gives ESAs to families making almost four times the poverty level. A family of five would qualify even with an income of over $110,000. Even under a proposed amendment, families at more than two-and-a-half times the poverty level could still get vouchers.

Furthermore, the bill ignores assets and wealth. The mega-rich could qualify for vouchers by any competent tax lawyer easily helping them defer or shelter income. Multibillionaire former governor Bill Haslam could qualify. (In fairness, Governor Haslam never supported a voucher plan to benefit wealthy families.)

Tell Legislators Not to Approve a Government Giveaway

By contrast, an elderly woman asking the state to help with her nursing home bills cannot have life savings of more than $2,000. But this bill would let even the richest Tennesseans qualify for an ESA voucher entitlement.

Proponents talk about poor students in struggling schools. But students in our biggest cities attending any public school, even the highest performing schools, would be entitled to a voucher.

Proponents are telling rural and suburban legislators the bill will not impact their districts. But sending tax dollars from suburban and rural areas to urban areas impacts everyone's district.

And vouchers always start in cities but then go statewide. New Orleans, Cleveland, and Milwaukee vouchers expanded to all of Louisiana, Ohio, and Wisconsin. Those pushing this legislation want vouchers all over Tennessee.

We believe Governor Lee genuinely wants to help the poor. But whoever drafted this legislation has failed to deliver on the governor's promises.

The General Assembly, with Governors Bredesen and Haslam, helped create America's fastest improving public schools. Why risk this progress by draining money out of public schools to further enrich the mega-rich?

Please tell your legislators and the governor to think again about creating another huge government giveaway, an entitlement in the name of the poor, benefiting the rich, at the expense of the taxpayers.

—"The Tennessee Education Savings Account Bill Fails the Math Test," *Commercial Appeal*, 9 April 2019.

PART 5. JUSTICE

11
ECONOMIC JUSTICE

In 2009 the federal minimum wage was set at $7.25 per hour. Over a decade later, despite legislative attempts to raise the minimum wage, the poorest working Tennesseans continue to make $7.25 an hour and income inequality has grown. The next essay addresses the minimum wage issue.

The second essay reflects on how the state's economic problems are especially painful in rural Tennessee.

RAISE MINIMUM WAGE AND FIGHT "INCOME INEQUALITY" (2014)

I commend Governor Bill Haslam for recently acknowledging that "income inequality" is a problem. Boy, is it.

In three decades, America's richest 1 percent saw their household incomes almost quadruple. The poorest working Americans saw a percentage increase of 16 percent, only a percentage increase of one-seventeenth as much as the rich.

In 1965, CEOs made twenty times more than the average worker. Today, CEOs make nearly three hundred times the pay of the average worker. The rising tide that once lifted all boats now lifts only yachts.

If the 1968 minimum wage of $1.60 an hour was merely adjusted for inflation, today it would be $10.74.

From 1968 to 2012, worker productivity rose 124 percent. If pay had kept pace with productivity, today the minimum wage would be $22.

Almost fifty studies have been published that found that, when the minimum wage goes up, poverty goes down. Raising the minimum wage to $10.10 per hour would give minimum wage workers an additional $5,700 per year, lifting nearly six million Americans out of poverty.

Tennessee leads the nation in the share of workers earning minimum wage, nearly twice the national average. And almost half of the states have a higher minimum wage than ours.

This year, Tennessee Democratic legislators proposed raising the minimum wage a dollar to $8.25 an hour. But Tea Party Republicans quickly killed the bill—even though Republican legislators have enjoyed not one but two pay hikes since the minimum wage was last raised.

Tea Party Republicans argue that increasing the minimum wage will force businesses to fire workers. In fact, 60 percent of the states that raised the minimum wage during periods of high unemployment saw higher-than-average job growth, not lower.

Many businesses support a higher minimum wage, including Costco, McDonald's, Subway, Panera Bread, Gap, and Stride Rite.

Tea Party Republicans argue that raising the minimum wage would hurt our economic recovery, but most economists believe the opposite. Raising the minimum wage would stimulate our economy and give consumer spending an immediate boost. Higher wages would give low-income workers the ability to purchase goods like food and cars that jump-start the economy. An increase in the minimum wage from $7.25 to $10.10 would grow the US economy by $22 billion and net 85,000 new jobs.

Raising the minimum wage would not increase costs significantly for consumers. Research shows that food price increases following an increase in the minimum wage will lead to no more than an extra dime a day for American households while delivering $35 billion in additional income to almost thirty million workers.

Furthermore, because the minimum wage is so low, we taxpayers fund a larger government safety net of food stamp programs, Medicaid, the Earned Income Tax Credit, and housing assistance. Raising the minimum wage would generate more taxes from workers, save the rest of us tax dollars, and reduce the deficit.

In 2007, when Republican President Bush advocated increasing the minimum wage from \$5.15 to \$7.25, thirty-nine current House Republicans and twenty-four current Senate Republicans voted to do so, including our own Senator Bob Corker and Senator Lamar Alexander.

Yet, this year when a Democratic president argued for raising the minimum wage, Republicans voted against it. Senator Alexander now even says he doesn't believe in the minimum wage and would abolish it.

If Governor Haslam is truly concerned about income inequality, and I believe he is, he should help solve the problem by raising the minimum wage.

> —Co-authored with Garrett Jennings and Hannah Oakley.
> "Raise Minimum Wage and Fight 'Income Inequality,'"
> *The Tennessean*, 28 June 2014.

WHAT WE ALL LOSE IN RURAL WEST TENNESSEE'S DECLINE (2017)

My family has been in West Tennessee since 1819. My multiple-greats grandfather and his brother-in-law were the first settlers in Weakley County. Soon he

The author's ancestor was one of the first two settlers in Weakley County, and his family has farmed there ever since. Here the author stands amid soybeans on the family farm. Photo: Bill Fletcher.

The author with two voters at an event during his first political campaign in 1986.
Photo property of author.

came in second only to his later-arrived neighbor Davy Crockett in bear killing,
or so said my mother and Goodspeed's 1887 *History of Tennessee*.

Seven generations of our family have lived here in West Tennessee. My
brother and I will be the last. My three sons are all grown and graduated from
college. All are working and studying in other places. They love their family
and friends here, the people who have blessed them so. But, like so many of
their talented friends, they will settle in the cities somewhere else.

As the *Commercial Appeal's* Tom Charlier reported earlier this month, West
Tennessee's population is in decline. Of the twenty-one counties in the region,
fifteen experienced declines since 2010. The region's overall population lost
nearly 1,200, while East and Middle Tennessee continued to grow.

West Tennessee's rural areas are hurting. Our leading exports are our jobs
and our young people.

I didn't vote for President Donald Trump, but I think I understand why
three-fourths of my neighbors did. They've seen their factory jobs sent to other
countries, their construction jobs taken by folks from other countries. They've
seen their children move to our cities if they're lucky and to other states if
they're not.

When candidate Trump promised to "build a wall" and "bring our jobs back," it sounded pretty good to so many who'd lost their jobs and their children.

I grew up down the street from the late Governor Ned McWherter. In his fourteen years as House Speaker and eight years as governor, and with the help of others like former Congressman John Tanner, Governor McWherter did a world of good for our area. We now have a four-lane highway through town, which intersects another new four-lane just six miles away, near the University of Tennessee at Martin. We have some incredible assets here, many of those through Governor McWherter's leadership.

In our town, I remember the shoe factory where Governor McWherter got his start and the boot factory that followed there. The women's clothing factory was followed in that building by an auto-parts manufacturer until it too closed. There was the factory that made wheels and the equipment manufacturer. The biggest of all was the book printing factory that employed nearly a thousand, not counting the book distribution plant near it.

I can remember when in our town of three thousand there were about that many factory jobs. All are gone. Until a manufactured housing plant burned in a nearby town and moved to Dresden, the largest private employer in our hometown was the supermarket. And if you could ship manufactured homes from China, I guess the supermarket would still be the business with the most employees.

Maybe NAFTA and the trade deals have been good for the world, and maybe they've been good for this nation overall. You can look to our nation's coasts and cities and make that case. But in the rural areas and in the South, especially here in West Tennessee where so many have paid for NAFTA with their jobs and without much to replace them, it's been tough. Really tough.

My family's been farming here since that grandfather in the early 1800s. Granddaddy and grandmama farmed full-time, Dad part-time, and I grew up working on our farm. I still remember the old houses where seven families lived on and worked our land. But modern agriculture is so amazingly productive today, farms that once employed seven families probably are not a seventh of one family farm today.

I look at the technological and scientific progress, and I know that is good in that all of us pay less for food than we would otherwise. But what about the people who no longer farm?

When our hometown invested in and fancied up the court square, every one of the construction workers (not counting a foreman) that I saw was from another country. I noticed but probably not like the folks who had lost their jobs on the farms and in the factories and in construction.

Governor McWherter often said, "Schools plus roads equal jobs." That was true thirty years ago, and it's still true today, but now "schools" means post-secondary higher education that prepares us for the higher-tech jobs of this new century. And "roads" today means broadband and high-speed internet highways that rural areas often lack. With wise investments in education and technology, our future can brighten again.

Rural Tennesseans have amazing assets and powerful strengths. We have families who love us before we're born and whose goodness continues to bless us even after they die.

We have neighbors who may not be blood kin but who care for us like we were. Neighbors who help raise us, know more about what we need than we do, and help us more than we can ask.

We have our churches (and a few synagogues) led by pastors and people whose hardships have forced them to their knees and their prayers to the heavens, and a good and gracious God still answers our prayers.

The author joined Governor McWherter, Congressman John Tanner, Greenfield Mayor Mike Biggs, and others in opening a new plant in the home county of Governor McWherter and the author. Photo: *Weakley County Press* and *Dresden Enterprise*.

Charlie Daniel and the author share a concern about jobs for our young people. The author has often emphasized in speeches that in rural Tennessee, "Our leading exports are our jobs and our young people. But we can return prosperity to the hurting rural areas of our state and our country if we make wise investments in education." Illustration by Charlie Daniel, *Knoxville News Sentinel*.

We have a powerful patriotism, led by more military and veterans per capita than anywhere else, strong in our belief in the high ideals that call this nation to fulfill the meaning of our creeds.

We have sacred values that come from families that love us, neighbors that bless us, and churches and schools that teach us. We believe that, if we love our neighbors and trust in our Creator, work hard and pray hard, God will continue to bless our people and these places we are blessed to call home.

—"What We All Lose in Rural West Tennessee's Decline,"
Commercial Appeal, 17 September 2017.

Governor McWherter emphasized his "95 county jobs" program. He frequently said that "schools plus roads equal jobs." Today those jobs require postsecondary education, and companies require access to high-speed "fiber" internet.

The challenges of meeting those needs in rural Tennessee continue and, if anything, grow harder. Shortly after his 2018 election, Governor Bill Lee appointed a talented West Tennessean, the Honorable Brandon Gibson, to lead his efforts to serve rural Tennessee. His first executive order required each state department to recommend how it could better serve rural citizens. Governor Lee has repeatedly talked about doing more for rural communities. In 2019, he convened a "Rural Opportunity Summit," a meeting of leaders from fifteen distressed counties. The *Tennessean* reports that "the executive order and recent summit demonstrates that rural issues maintain a major priority for Lee."[1]

1   Natalie Allison, "Governor Bill Lee, took his cabinet to rural Tennessee, where local leaders asked for their help. *The Tennessean*, August 19, 2019.

12
PREDATORY LENDING

Israel's laws long forbade the exaction of interest from a poor person and required a creditor to return before sundown a neighbor's garment that had been pledged (see Exodus 22:25–27).

In ancient times, commercial relations were comparatively undeveloped, but loans were commonly needed for the purpose of relieving distress. To exact interest from a borrower who was reduced to poverty by misfortune and debt was to gain from a neighbor's need. Thus, the Pentateuch, the first five books of the Hebrew Bible, condemned the charging of interest from fellow Israelites (see Deuteronomy 23:19–20).

Despite Nehemiah's and Ezekiel's calls for strict observance of these laws, violations were frequent (see Nehemiah 5:6–13; Ezekiel 18:8–17; 22:12). The practice of Israelites lending to fellow Israelites at exorbitant rates became "a social plague" that made debtors' situations practically hopeless.

Today, poor and indebted Americans are the victims of a similar social plague. Predatory lending frequently and repeatedly abuse working people and senior citizens.

We often complain of being overregulated, and in some areas we are.

But the Bible is filled with regulations about how people should deal with each other—including economic regulations—in order to live justly.

For most of Tennessee's history, our Constitution and laws have limited interest and prohibited usury. But today meaningful limits are only history.

The next op-eds were written to advocate on behalf of Tennessee's most economically disadvantaged citizens. Our poorer citizens now too often are the victims of high interest rates and excessive fees imposed by predatory lenders burying borrowers in insurmountable debt. The following essays push for reforms to prevent citizens from being exploited.

CREDIT CARD SHOWER NO BLESSING (1985)

"Debt-free folks just aren't to be trusted." That was the title of a recent column by Chicago journalist Mike Royko. Royko told of a friend who received a flattering letter from the Visa credit card folks. They offered him, "one of a very select group of people," a Citibank Preferred Visa Card.

The Chicagoan applied for the card modestly touted as "the best credit card in the world." There was just one problem: he had paid for his home twenty years earlier and had paid cash for both of his cars. Because he did not owe anybody and he had not owed anybody for years, the Visa people rejected his application. Visa stated its reasoning this way: "an insufficient number of satisfactory references in your creditor report."

This would-be debtor was unsure what he would do next. "Maybe I'll have to go into debt so that they will trust me."

The same day I read about this, a couple came to my law office to talk about bankruptcy.

Like Royko's friend, some months earlier they had received a letter asking them to apply for a Visa card. Unlike Royko's friend, they were already living beyond their means on other credit cards and owed several debts. Thus, they qualified for and soon received a Visa card.

Then the next Visa solicitation letter came. They also completed that form and soon had their second Visa card. That was nice, since they were moving toward the credit limit on the first card.

A third Visa solicitation letter arrived. By now they were getting the hang of filling out those applications. Then came the fourth solicitation letter from a Visa bank. Then the fifth. The sixth. The seventh.

They soon proudly possessed—or were possessed by—seven Visa cards and $15,000 of debt. Quite frankly, as I counsel clients, I often discourage them from taking bankruptcy. Part of my reluctance is that I think you ought to pay your debts if you can. It's an old-fashioned notion, to be sure, but one still widely held here in rural Tennessee.

Fortunately for the Visa banks and other creditors, this couple wants to pay their debts. So, I'm writing letters to the Visa people suggesting they stop harassing these folks through computer-generated letters that demand larger payments and offer more credit cards.

I think the creditors will cooperate. It's like Senator Al Gore, Jr. (D-TN) observed the other day when discussing the enormous debts owed by other countries to American banks. "If you owe the bank a little, *you* have problem. If you owe the bank a lot, the *bank* has a problem."

Visa has a problem.

Part of Visa's problem, however, is not with "deadbeat" debtors. It's with its own deadbeats, those whose hearts don't beat at all—those amazing computers that send out millions of solicitation letters.

Like Visa, many others of us in business also have problems with persons not paying bills. Unlike the computers, we sometimes have soft hearts—or, like Visa, we have avaricious appetites for sales and business and extend easy credit to persons who cannot afford what they want.

I once sat on the board of directors of a savings and loan association, an institution so small and a board of directors so conservative that we directors considered each application for a home loan.

Often loan applicants would have enough savings for a sizable down payment and were purchasing a fine home. Even if later they had not made the payments and we had to foreclose, the savings and loan would not have lost any money. Still, we rejected many of those applications.

Why?

"You're not doing this couple any favor to make them this loan," Richard Maloan, a wise and experienced director, would say. "You'll be doing them a favor not to put them so deep in debt that they can't make it."

Those of us working in and for American businesses need to listen to Richard Maloan.

So do Congress and President Reagan.

I think Mike Royko and his Chicago friend already have.

—"Credit Card Shower No Blessing,"
Commercial Appeal, 10 July 1985.

RESIST LOBBYISTS AND CRACK DOWN ON PREDATORY LENDING (2004)

I know of a hard-working Memphis couple. She works at a hospital, and her husband is a barber. They decided to purchase a home for $65,000, but by the time their lender finished adding on fees and other charges, they were looking at first and second mortgages totaling $91,000.

The day they were to close the loans, they loaded their belongings in a U-Haul truck, but the lender delayed the closing. They found a place to stay the night with their two sons and waited until the new closing time, at 4 p.m. the next day. That was when they learned the interest rates on their loans would be much higher than expected—15 percent for the first mortgage and 29 percent for the second. But with their belongings and their children waiting in the truck and no other place to live, they signed the documents.

Another Memphian, an elderly woman, owed $5,000 on her home. Although she did not need a loan, a finance company persuaded her to borrow $35,000 against her home at 18 percent interest. Included in the loan was a $6,000 credit life insurance premium and more than $2,000 in loan origination fees. Her loan is negatively amortized, so after six years of paying $500 monthly notes, she owes more than the amount she borrowed.

Predatory lenders like the ones who victimized these people are not just a Memphis problem, and they are not just an urban problem. They are a problem all across Tennessee and one the legislature needs to deal with.

I first learned of predatory lending from a country lawyer in rural West Tennessee who represents banks, other financial enterprises, and real estate agents at loan closings. He said trusting, honest people were being victimized and something should be done to outlaw the unconscionable terms he was seeing at loan closings.

For at least five decades, my family has helped people borrow money to buy homes. My father co-founded a financial institution to make home loans. My father and I served on its board. My wife served six years as the chair of the board of a multi-billion-dollar bank that helps other banks make home loans.

Lending money to help someone buy a home can be noble work. But lending money to take someone's home is dastardly.

The General Assembly's Joint Predatory Lending Study Committee held hearings across the state in 2002 and last year. Testimony from Chattanooga to Memphis documented that predatory home mortgage lending has become a statewide problem. Yet for the third straight year, powerful lobbyists blocked bills to crack down on abusive practices in the lending industry.

This year, the Bredesen administration may act on the issue, though it is not yet clear whether its proposals will be strong enough to prevent such abuses.

Predatory home mortgage lenders prey on those least able to decipher complex loan documents, least likely to seek out reputable lenders, and least likely to have the means to address financial problems once they begin. A large percentage of their victims are uneducated, minorities, disabled, or elderly.

Such predators use deceptive tactics to sell loans and high-pressure tactics to prevent victims from properly scrutinizing their terms. They conduct closing procedures in homes or in a hurry and work with unscrupulous real estate agents, appraisers, and contractors to take advantage of victims.

Testimony and reports gathered in our hearings revealed that predatory lending involves home mortgages, mortgage refinancing, home equity loans, and home repair loans with extremely high interest rates, excessive fees, balloon payments, prepayment penalties, and the imposition of other questionable and sometimes fraudulent terms. Such loans have grown rapidly in low-income neighborhoods, often stripping away assets that may have taken owners decades or a lifetime to accumulate.

Whether meaningful reform occurs this year depends on whether the voices of citizens can be heard over the roars of the powerful interests that make millions of dollars from practices such as these:

- Excessive mortgage broker compensation. In the subprime market, some brokers attempt to sell borrowers a loan with the most fees and the highest interest rate possible to make more money for themselves.
- Excessive points and fees, well above the normal 1 percent origination fee, 1 percent of the loan amount in points and basic closing costs.
- Debt consolidation home equity loans that trade short-term for long-term debt. Some debt consolidation loans take fifteen to thirty years to pay off and cost much more in interest payments.
- Huge balloon payments that are due at the end of the loan repayment term, usually after fifteen years. If a borrower is elderly, it may be difficult to refinance the loan when the balloon payment comes due and foreclosure may be inevitable.
- Equity stripping. An unscrupulous lender may lend an amount that is more than the borrower can handle, knowing he or she is likely to default. The lender can then foreclose and sell the house.
- Flipping, the repeated refinancing of a loan. A predatory lender may encourage a consumer to refinance to get a little more cash out of his or her available equity. Each time, more fees are charged, placing the borrower deeper in debt over a longer period.

- Insurance packing, adding unwanted extras such as credit life or disability insurance to a loan.
- Home improvement contractors who act as loan originators or mortgage brokers and assist low-income homeowners in borrowing funds from mortgage lenders for repairs. State laws exempt home improvement contractors from mortgage broker licensing laws, enabling them to perform such activities without the risk of penalties.

—"Resist Lobbyists and Crack Down on Predatory Lending,"
Commercial Appeal, 11 January 2004.

"TITLE PLEDGE LENDING" MUST BE CHANGED (2007)

Anita Gray was hurting. Our fellow Tennessean was raising her two young grandchildren but could not make ends meet. Then she borrowed $1,000, which made things better—for thirty days.

But after a month, she owed the original $1,000 plus another $220!

Anita Gray had borrowed from a "title pledge lender" at the legal effective interest rate—22 percent per month, 264 percent per year.

Mind you, the law says the "interest" is only 2 percent per month, or 24 percent per year. But that same squalid law allows another 20 percent per month—240 percent per year—for an "administration fee."

In eighteen months, this forty-year-old working woman paid over $4,000—and still owed more than when she started! On a $1,000 loan, she paid more than $4,000 in eighteen months and still owed $1,200. How can that be?

To begin, the 264 percent per year on $1,000 for eighteen months comes to $3,960. In addition, lenders often charge other fees and "expenses."

Unfortunately, Ms. Gray is one of thousands of working Tennesseans who suffer from what we used to call "loan-sharking" but is now called "title pledge lending."

Abuses Taint Good System

Mind you, we believe lending people money can be good, and most lenders are honorable professionals. In fact, our families have made much of our living in the community lending business.

Furthermore, we believe strongly in the free enterprise system and are blessed to participate in it as businessmen. Our free enterprise system is the finest on earth, and we give thanks for it.

But for two hundred years, our American free enterprise system did not allow the poor to be preyed upon in these ways. Until a few years ago, there was a cap on interest of 10 percent. Times changed, and the constitutional cap came off—and should have. But then the laws were changed further, some traditional lenders stopped making small loans, new entities were created, and unprecedented abuses began.

It is one thing to charge more on risky loans that require much work. But title pledge lenders only loan up to 30 percent of the value of the vehicle. In other words, on a $10,000 car, they would lend no more than $3,000. They are very secured lenders, not unsecured.

We know that trucks and cars crash and disappear. Still, at current rates, if a borrower only pays fees and interest—no principal—for just five months, the lender gets their money back plus an annualized return of over 20 percent.

Mind you, the rich preying on, instead of praying with, the poor is an issue as ancient as Scripture. That is why Old Testament law prohibits lending practices now common in Tennessee. That is why the Hebrew prophets like Hosea, Amos, and Micah raged against injustices done to God's people.

Today, we ought to rage against the injustices being done to Tennessee's people. And the General Assembly should change the law so that working people find less loan-sharking and more reasonable rates.

—Co-authored with Representative Craig Fitzhugh.
"'Title Pledge Lending' Must Be Changed,"
The Tennessean, 23 February 2007.

PART 6. LEADERSHIP

From left: The author, Vice President Al Gore, and Governor Ned McWherter. Photo property of the author.

13
OUR LEADING LEADERS

Tennessee has been fortunate to have extraordinary political leaders. In the second half of the twentieth century, Governor Frank Clement and Senators Estes Kefauver and Albert Gore, Sr., all were Democrats considered for President or Vice President. Republican senators Howard Baker, Lamar Alexander, and Fred Thompson all ran for President. Albert Gore, Jr., served eight years as vice president and in 2000 won the popular vote for President though he narrowly lost the Electoral College in that still-controversial election.

Democratic senator Jim Sasser was about to become the majority leader of the US Senate before a Republican tidal wave elected Senator Bill Frist. Then soon Senator Frist became the Senate Majority Leader.

All of these leaders, and many others, were and are highly esteemed. But none are held in higher regard than Governor Ned McWherter and Senator Howard Baker. Both deserve our highest respect. The following two essays applaud Tennessee's greatest Democratic governor and greatest Republican national leader.

The first essay was taken from a speech made in Governor McWherter's

and my hometown of Dresden at a traveling exhibit of Tennessee's history
and people.

The second essay was a review of a book about Senator Howard Baker.

A "TENNESSEE TREASURE" (1994)

At this "Tennessee Treasures" exhibit you will learn of historic leaders. But what
about the one who brought the exhibit to us, who served the last twenty-two
years as Speaker of the House and governor?

When future historians create another exhibit, what will they say about Ned
McWherter's years as governor?

Strongest economy. Historians should note that, for the first time in history, Tennessee's economy was rated "the strongest in the South." That's what
Dow Jones said, and the Corporation for Enterprise Development ranked our
economy not only "the best in the South" but also "the fifth strongest in the
nation."

Most jobs. But when Ned McWherter became governor, almost half our
counties—forty-two out of ninety-five—had double-digit unemployment. As
a candidate for governor in 1986, Speaker McWherter talked about a "ninety-
five-county jobs program." And he had one. Now Tennessee has the lowest
unemployment since we started keeping records. Instead of forty-two counties
with 10 percent or more unemployment, today there is but one.

Better education. This self-described "college drop-out," whose two children
and their spouses earned nine university degrees, including three doctorates,
saw education as crucial to our economy and our children's future.

He promised his second term was "for the kids"—and it was.

He took our schools back from the courts and gave them to the kids in a
way that children, especially rural children, had never had them. He created a
funding mechanism that finally is fairer to rural schools while he helped urban
schools, too.

In the last three years, Tennessee's K–12 schools have had the nation's greatest
growth in state funding, an increase of 49 percent. Our Twenty-First Century
Schools program has put those dollars directly into classrooms to buy textbooks
and computers and add teachers, investing more than three times as much in
classroom improvements in three years as was spent the previous sixteen years.

With historic classroom funding has come historic accountability. For the
first time, all school boards are elected by the people and accountable directly
to the citizens. Tennessee taxpayers can see schools' strengths and weaknesses

in published report cards. In another first, Tennessee leads the nation with a new system measuring how much students learn.

Record roads. There was another crucial part to Governor McWherter's economic development plan. As he often says, "schools plus roads equal jobs." As speaker and governor, he created and carried out the largest road-building program in Tennessee history. A thousand miles of roads.

Middle Tennessee long has enjoyed its three interstates, as has East Tennessee, while West Tennessee had only I-40. Governor McWherter once noted that every governor is accused of building roads in his home area and, if he was going to be accused, he sure wanted to be guilty! So now, instead of riding back roads, West Tennessee is becoming a crossroads.

It is true all across Tennessee. A man born near Palmersville and from Dresden knew we had to connect rural counties to city neighbors, to the commerce and opportunities of this entire country. Now all of us, country and city alike, benefit. Schools and roads have equaled jobs.

Criminal justice. Before Ned McWherter became governor, the prisons had exploded in riots and escapes. Inmates and a federal judge had taken over.

To control criminals and protect Tennesseans, Governor McWherter built six prisons with seven thousand beds. He built more cells than all the governors since the Depression—combined.

His high-tech prison management system cut operating costs in new prisons by almost half (46 percent). Today Tennessee has the only fully accredited prison system in the country. He's taken control of the prisons back from criminals and courts.

Governor McWherter also enabled this century's only comprehensive revision of our criminal code, making protection from violent criminals the first priority. Under his administration the legislature created the punishment of life without parole, which makes a life sentence mean exactly that.

Our families are never as safe as we want, but they are much safer because of these enormous changes in criminal justice.

Better health care. Ned McWherter knew our families were threatened by killers, not only criminals but also killing diseases and illnesses. And our state budget was threatened by a Medicaid system with costs soaring totally out of control.

We had three options: (1) continue a government-dictated Medicaid system that either was going to suck hundreds of millions of dollars from schools, drive taxes out of sight, or both; (2) make catastrophic cuts in coverage for our neediest children, women, and senior citizens; or (3) invest in radical reform.

Tennessee in a year has done what Washington talks about doing in a decade. Washington aims for 95 percent of our citizens to have health insurance in the next millennium. Tennessee will achieve it next month.

To get that coverage, Washington talks about employer mandates; Tennessee did it without them. Washington talks about government cost controls, while Tennessee slows spiraling costs with reasonable reforms and free-market competition. Other states aren't calling on Washington to lead; they're calling Tennessee and asking how they can follow our lead.

Is everything perfect with TennCare? Certainly not. Federal bureaucrats blocked reforms the governor wanted while a year's experience shows other changes we now can implement. But is Tennessee better off than if we had kept Medicaid? Tennessee taxpayers sure are. So are 390,000 members of working families who could not afford health insurance before but who have it now. So are former welfare mothers who no longer have to choose between a job and health care for their kids but now can afford TennCare and are working taxpayers instead of tax-takers.

Lowest taxes. What's all this costing us? What's the bottom line on taxes after Governor McWherter? Tennesseans now pay less in state and local taxes per $100 of personal income than citizens in any other state.

That's right. When you look at our income and our taxes, our combined state and local tax burden is fiftieth of fifty states.

Lower debt. If our taxes are the lowest, then did Governor McWherter finance these changes like Washington with enormous deficits, or like states with ballooning bond debts?

No. He balanced all eight budgets. The state's bonded indebtedness, when adjusted for inflation and measured in real dollars, is substantially lower than when he took office. Furthermore, he'll leave a record "rainy day fund," probably triple what it was when he took office.

Then how did he do it?

Best management. The last two years *City and State* magazine recognized Tennessee as "the best managed state in the nation." Number one among fifty.

Decades in business and eighteen years in the legislature, including a record fourteen as House Speaker, made Ned McWherter the most experienced governor Tennessee ever chose. He really did only need "a cup of coffee and four vanilla wafers" before he was ready to work.

And work he did. He and his team worked like heck from early till late, with weekdays and weekends blurring together.

Governor McWherter is the first to give credit to others for Tennessee's historic records and national marks in jobs, economic growth, education, roads, criminal justice, health care, and managing state government. But he was the leader, the chief executive who knew how to work with the General Assembly, his cabinet and state workers, private citizens, and all of Tennessee.

He is right to say Tennesseans accomplished these things together. But we are right to say that few, if any, of these achievements would have happened without his leadership.

Now *Governing* magazine has judged Ned McWherter the nation's best governor.

When historians put together the next exhibit of Tennessee treasures, they ought to recognize that America's best governor today, and the best governor in Tennessee's first two hundred years, was our own Ned McWherter.

—"A 'Tennessee Treasure,'"
Commercial Appeal, 25 December 1994.

I acknowledge I am biased about Governor McWherter. Our families have been close for at least three generations. I grew up down the street from him. When I was finishing college, he was kind to let me work for him and the Tennessee House of Representatives in Nashville. When he ran for governor, I wanted to follow his leadership, and I was fortunate to follow in representing his House seat.

I am *biased* about Governor McWherter but *not prejudiced.*

I did not pre-judge him. I did not reach the above conclusions before he served as Speaker of the House of Representatives and especially as governor. I had the extraordinary privilege of watching him and his team work as I served in the Tennessee House during his eight years as governor.

Tennessee has been fortunate to have many honest and good governors. But I sincerely doubt that historians, public administration professors, and knowledgeable observers of either party will conclude that Tennessee has had another governor who accomplished as much or did as well for our citizens as Governor Ned R. McWherter.

BOOK REVIEW OF *HOWARD BAKER: CONCILIATOR IN AN AGE OF CRISIS* (1998)

Former United States Senator Howard Baker probably has done more for Republicans than any other Tennessean. But even though I am a Democrat, I have long admired and respected him. This book only increases that respect.

At a time when strident, take-no-prisoners partisanship in Congress seems to have reached record levels, one especially appreciates Howard Baker's bi-partisan cooperation.

Granted, Senator Baker could be partisan as a candidate. His partisanship, however, certainly was not like today's mean-spirited, vicious attacks that characterize fellow Americans as enemies and seek to divide our country.

The overriding theme of this biography is that Howard Baker was a "conciliator," someone who tried to work with persons of different views and values, different perspectives and parties. He tried to build consensus, or at least working majorities, for good legislation to pass and for government to serve people.

Baker's skills as an attorney helping resolve conflicts are demonstrated repeatedly. One sees why he became the most famous Tennessee attorney of his generation.

Time and again, Howard Baker did the right thing in difficult circumstances. Whether it was the Panama Canal treaty ratification or the Watergate investigation into his own party's White House wrongs, Baker rose above petty partisanship and shallow sloganeering and did what he believed was right.

J. Lee Annis, Jr., a college professor in Maryland, wrote this book from his 900-page dissertation. Fortunately, it now is but 216 pages, plus 61 pages of notes, bibliography, and index.

A Republican who is a devout Baker supporter recently told me he found the book too one-sided, as though the Senator was without human shortcomings. Perhaps Professor Annis does not seek to make criticisms that should be made.

But unquestionably Senator Baker served our state and country extraordinarily well both in the Senate and as presidential chief of staff. The book is not great, but it is about a great man. It is interesting and well worth reading.

Those of us privileged to serve the public, whether in elected office or as officers of the courts, should model our service after the best public servants, both Democrats and Republicans. Howard Baker's service to Tennessee and America represents public service in its most productive and intellectually honest form.

—Book Review of J. Lee Annis, Jr.,
Howard Baker: Conciliator in an Age of Crisis,
in *Tennessee Bar Journal*, July/August 1998.

To many today, Senator Howard Baker and his bipartisanship seem out-of-date, even antiquated. But when one looks at what Senator Baker accomplished and what he enabled Congress and Presidents to accomplish, one sees a compelling case for America to return to his timeless and truly patriotic values.

The most readable and finest biography on Senator Baker was written by a Memphian and, interestingly, a Democrat, Bill Haltom. Bill's late mother-in-law, Claude Swafford, was one of very few women in Senator Baker's law school class at the University of Tennessee. The future Senator soon became great friends with the highly intelligent, beautiful and charming Claude and another talented classmate, Claude's future husband Howard Swafford. Through Claude Swafford, her son-in-law was able to interview Senator Baker and with his help interview many of the Senator's friends. Regardless of your politics, Bill Haltom's *The Other Fellow May Be Right* is well worth reading. And the life of Senator Baker is well worth studying—and emulating.

14
CHRISTIAN DEMOCRATS

"How can you be a Democrat? Weren't you a minister, and aren't you a Christian?"

I have heard these questions repeatedly, especially since recently becoming chairman of the Tennessee Democratic Party. While I pray with, respect, and love many faithful Republicans, I am a Democrat, not despite being a Christian but because I am a Christian.

I'm a Democrat because I believe in Jesus's Golden Rule ("Do unto others as you would have them do unto you") instead of the politician's Golden Rule ("Those with the gold make the rules"). I'm a Democrat because John 3:16 teaches, "For God so loved the world"—not just the powerful or the powerless, not just those who look like us or think like us, but the whole world.

I'm a Democrat because I believe Americans are family and because of what Americans have done for my family.

I'm a Democrat because after my father was gravely wounded in World War II, programs sponsored by Democrats saved his life with medical care, and the GI Bill helped that disabled veteran rehabilitate, attend university, and learn a profession. I'm a Democrat because my father, as a judge, taught me that politicians should not limit people's access to the courts, citizen juries, and justice, but there should be personal responsibility for all and immunity for none.

I'm a Democrat because, as the husband of the first woman graduate of the Vanderbilt Law and Divinity program and the first woman attorney in private practice in our county, I know Democrats have fought for equal opportunities for our wives, sisters, and daughters.

I'm a Democrat because I believe in the work my engineer brother, engineer nephew, and engineer niece have done on Democrat-sponsored research and development projects that help make America the world's most advanced, strongest, and most secure country.

I'm a Democrat because my family hunts and fishes and enjoys God's creation that Democrats protect through conservation laws preserving clean water and air and saving our children from cancer-causing chemicals and poisonous pollutants.

I'm a Democrat because Dr. Sal Lombardi, a high-risk pregnancy specialist, used his expertise developed through Democrat-created educational opportunities to save our twin sons.

I'm a Democrat because I believe in the public schools and teachers that educated our sons and make a difference in the lives of Tennesseans. I'm a Democrat because I believe in the work my sister did as a special education teacher, helping children become taxpayers instead of tax-takers.

I'm a Democrat because I hate debt (my pickup has almost 500,000 miles, but it's paid for).[1] The last three Republican presidents set world records for deficits, Clinton-Gore achieved record surpluses, and now the Republican House refuses to work with its leadership and the president to stop piling debt on our children.

I'm a Democrat because I believe not in atheist Ayn Rand's gospel of selfishness but in Christ's Gospel of service, knowing that Matthew 25 teaches that nations will be judged by how we treat "the least of these."

In a time when our state and nation have gone from common sense to nonsense, it's past time we returned to values America has held dear. In our Ameri-

---

1   That truck now has over 550,000 miles and we still use it, though my mechanic has told me, "Roy, I don't mind towing you—it's easy work and good money. But you better not take that truck outside this county any more."

can family, we have many faiths, but our shared values led me to the Tennessee Democratic Party. I hope you will join us.

—"Strong Faith Led to Democratic Party,"
Knoxville News Sentinel, knoxnews.com, 2 March 2013.
A similar essay was published in *The Tennessean* on February 20, 2013.

WHY I AM A DEMOCRAT (2012)

The *Christian Lawyer* asked that I tell you why I am both a Christian and a Democrat. Though honored to share with you, I am mindful of a remark attributed to Thomas Jefferson. President Jefferson reportedly said that, the more his dinner guest professed his honesty, the more Jefferson counted his silver.

Similarly, the more politicians publicly profess their faith, the more we should "count our silver." So, if you are skeptical of elected officials or yours truly, I understand your skepticism. And I encourage it!

But I am honored to share why I am a Democrat, though I do so mindful of what the Apostle Paul wrote to the Galatians: "There is neither Jew nor Greek, there is neither bond nor free, there is neither male nor female: for ye are all one in Christ Jesus."

Today Paul might write to the Americans: "There is neither poor nor rich, there is neither black nor white, there is neither male nor female, there is neither Democrat nor Republican: for you are all one in Christ Jesus."

Jesus exemplified, Paul taught, and the Scriptures proclaim that we are one in Christ Jesus.

I have known unity with dear Republican brothers and sisters as we have worked together through the years. Such unity has been important as we have wrestled with legislation and tried to do right. Unfortunately, today even in Tennessee and certainly in Washington, such unity is, at best, in short supply.

The Word is clear: what divides us is not nearly as important as what unites us. At a time of extreme partisanship, what America needs most from Christians is love. We need Christians who love our fellow Americans more than we hate the other political party.

Preaching "Bad News"

Unfortunately, too many preachers proclaim not the Good News but the Bad. Some preachers and Sunday school teachers tell congregations and classes that they cannot be Christians and Democrats. From their pulpit they preach and from their lectern they teach: "Christians cannot be Democrats!" Partisan preachers and some politicians have chosen not the Lord's work but one party's work. They have made Christians believe that Democrats do *not* believe.

Some preachers offer radical right-wing rhetoric that blesses the rich and damns the poor, which follows atheist Ayn Rand's gospel of selfishness rather than Christ's gospel of sacrifice. That philosophy contradicts the prayerful Republican President Abraham Lincoln while in effect proclaiming principles "with malice for many and charity for few."

But I am a Democrat not *despite* being a Christian but *because* I am a Christian.

Sacred Scripture

I'm a Democrat because I believe in those first words from America's sacred document, our Constitution, which begins, "We the People."

I'm a Democrat because I believe in Jesus's Golden Rule ("Do unto others as you would have them do unto you") instead of the politicians' Golden Rule ("Those with the gold make the rules").

John 3:16 and First John 3:16

I'm a Democrat because I am inspired by John 3:16, which begins, "For God so loved the world . . ."

"God so loved the *world*"—not just the Republicans or just the Democrats, not only the rich or the poor, not just the powerful or the powerless, but the whole world. That's who God loves. And that's what John 3:16 teaches.

And I'm a Democrat because I'm inspired not only by John 3:16 but also by verses beginning at *First* John 3:16 that teach us this:

"We know love by this, that he laid down his life for us—and we ought to lay down our lives for one another."

"But whosoever hath this world's goods, and seeth his brother have need, and shutteth up his bowels of compassion from him, how dwelleth the love of God in him?"

"My little children, let us not love in word, neither in tongue; but in deed and in truth."[2]

I'm a Democrat because I believe we are called to act when we see others in need.

---

2   1 John 3:16-18, King James Version (KJV).

Our American Family

I'm a Democrat because I believe Americans are family and because of what has happened to my family. I know what America has done for those I love and for so many other American families.

I'm a Democrat because, during the Great Depression, when my grandparents and so many Americans could not get enough for their crops to pay their bills, President Roosevelt and the Democratic Congress brought the New Deal, and farmers finally made enough to save their farms and feed our people.

I'm a Democrat because, when my father and many other brave warriors were gravely wounded in World War II, programs proposed and passed by Democrats saved their lives with medical care, and the GI Bill helped my disabled veteran father rehabilitate himself, go to university, and learn a profession.

I'm a Democrat because my father, as a judge, taught me that the courts belong not only to the rich but also to the poor and that the citizens serving as jurors should not be denied the power to hear cases and do justice. Yet today, Republican politicians limit people's access to the courts, citizen juries, and justice. I believe in personal responsibility for all and immunity for none, that wrongdoers should be held accountable, and that my Republican friends are wrong to immunize those who negligently harm victims.

I'm a Democrat because, as the husband of the first woman graduate of Vanderbilt Law and Divinity program and the first woman attorney in private practice in our county, I know Democrats created equal access to opportunities and freedoms for our sisters, wives, and daughters.

I'm a Democrat because my ninety-five-year-old mother's friends have been sustained during their senior years through Social Security, a program created by Democrats. My mother and other seniors have survived only through the health care provided by Medicare, another program created by Democrats.

I'm a Democrat because I believe in the work my engineer brother, nephew, and niece have done on Democrat-sponsored and taxpayer-funded research and development defense projects that have made America the most advanced, the strongest, and the most secure country on earth.

I'm a Democrat because I believe in the work that my sister did as a special education teacher with children born in poverty, through no fault of their own, and who too often are left to fend for themselves.

Our Babies

I'm a Democrat because the education, research, and health care programs that Democrats created saved my twin sons. A specialist told us the twins in my wife's womb would not survive and recommended, twice, that we abort. But a high-risk pregnancy specialist named Dr. Sal Lombardi made it possible for our twins' birth day not to be their death day. Dr. Lombardi knew what was possible because this man of faith graduated from public schools, went to college and medical school on federally subsidized student loans, and then developed his extraordinary expertise by learning from taxpayer-funded teachers, at government-funded universities, and hospitals. Each of his opportunities were made possible by Democrat-created programs. Treatment techniques, procedures, and medicines that helped save our babies (and literally hundreds of thousands of others) were developed through the research and programs that Democrats created and funded. Simply put, if not for the wise and compassionate decisions of men and women in government, most of those leaders being Democrats, and for the tax dollars paid by Democrats and Republicans alike, my sons would have died.

Bad Debt

I'm a Democrat because I believe in paying for what we spend instead of piling trillions in debt on the backs of our children. I've watched in recent decades as Republican administrations (President Reagan and the first President Bush) created the largest deficits in the history of the country. Then, the next Democratic administration (Clinton-Gore) helped this country have record surpluses, only to see the last Republican administration (Bush-Cheney) create new records for the largest deficits in history. It is right to give some blame to the Democrats who went along with the Bush-Cheney administration, but that administration created more national debt than all of the administrations in the history of the country. And they plunged us into the Great Recession, a recession so deep that those deficits have continued far too deeply and far too long in the same sorry course. Now, I watch a Republican House of Representatives refuse to cooperate even with its own Republican leadership, the Republicans in the Senate, and Democrats in the White House to fix the problem of our growing national debt.

Matthew 25

If those of us who profess to be Christians were as faithful and selfless as Jesus calls us to be, we would not need government. If the church were really The

Church, then the government could be limited to national defense and a few areas like transportation. But until that time, I am a Democrat because of Jesus's teachings in Matthew 25 in the passage known as "The Judgment of the Nations."

And how are nations to be judged?

By the way we treat those Jesus called "the least of these": the hungry, the thirsty, the stranger, the naked, the sick, and the poor. Democrats have led the way by, not perfectly, but repeatedly, feeding the hungry, cleaning our waters so all God's children can drink, clothing the naked children, and seeing that the sick have health care.

Class Warfare

Some of my Republican friends will charge—as some Republicans often charge—that Democrats engage in "class warfare." Unfortunately, I'm afraid that far too often Democrats do *not* engage when the super-rich engage in class warfare against working people and children.

Why is it only "class warfare" when Democrats defend working people and children from the crushing debt made more gigantic by huge tax breaks for Republican billionaires? Why is it not "class warfare" when Republican policies promote more wealth for the wealthiest and less for the middle class and vulnerable poor children?

The famous humorist and common-sense philosopher Will Rogers once observed, "I am not a member of any organized political party—I'm a Democrat." Similarly, I find myself not always agreeing with the policies of national Democrats. I am more a Southern Democrat. I described myself as a "compassionate conservative" before the second President Bush adopted the term.

I am a Democrat because some people have been kicked around and beaten down but could yet rise and stand on their own feet if we will but give them not a handout but a hand up.

I am a Democrat because the Hebrew laws, the eighth-century prophets, Jesus's teaching, and the apostles' preaching all require us to seek justice, do mercy, and love our neighbors. Even and especially those who are hurting the most and are the most vulnerable.

I am a Democrat because those of us who have been blessed the most have a special responsibility to serve the least and the last.

My parents taught me that the Democratic Party is the party of the willing and the working, the vulnerable and the valiant, the hurting and the helping. That's why I'm a Democrat. And why some of you are, too. And it is why others of you might want to think about joining us.

May your faith be strong, may your love embrace *all* of God's children, may you serve "the least of these," may both our political parties do what God calls us to do, and may God bless America.

—"Why I Am a Democrat,"
Christian Lawyer, Spring 2012.

I know that some Democrats would not be happy, and some Republicans would be absolutely irate, if I wrote an op-ed on "Why I Could Be a Republican." But I *could* write such an essay.

That essay would not describe the Tea Party Republicanism that recently has hijacked and dominated the nation's and Tennessee's Republican Party. It would describe the Republicanism of many of my colleagues from rural East Tennessee and of Senator Howard Baker. It would be an endorsement of the Republicanism of Abraham Lincoln, Teddy Roosevelt, Dwight Eisenhower, and Howard Baker—leaders who put their nation and its future first.

President Lincoln believed in the sacredness of national unity and was willing to fight a terrible war to save it and us. He grew to recognize that slavery was wrong and ultimately declared the Emancipation Proclamation. His poetic words at Gettysburg and his second inaugural address on the walls of the Lincoln Memorial inspire many of us still.

President Teddy Roosevelt fought for the working men and women, instituted protections for them and for our children, limited the power of those who would oppress Americans and pillage and plunder our people, and became the nation's leading conservationist.

President Eisenhower recognized that a national investment was needed to build our interstate system and insightfully said in 1954: "Should any political party attempt to abolish social security, unemployment insurance and eliminate labor laws and farm programs, you would not hear of that party again in our political history. There is a tiny splinter group, of course, that believes that you can do these things. Among them are a few Texas oil millionaires, and an occasional politician or businessman from other areas. Their number is negligible and they are stupid."

Senator Baker supported Civil Rights, respected the Constitution, fought against soaring national debt, and worked well with people of good faith in both parties.

My mentor, Governor McWherter, admired and worked cooperatively with Senator Baker. As Speaker of the House, Ned McWherter also worked closely with then Governor Alexander for what was best for Tennessee. Their differences in party did not prevent them from working together for our state. Speaker McWherter also worked with Congressman Jimmy Quillen of Tennessee's First Congressional District to bring health care to East Tennessee, quite a contrast with too many Tea Party Republicans who will let their hospitals close before they will accept federal funding to help their poorest neighbors and the working women and men of their districts.

When I served in the legislature, I sought votes from colleagues in both parties. And I quickly learned it often was easier to get along with my Republican friends than with my fellow Democrats since we were not so directly in competition for the same offices and opportunities. On many issues, often rural West Tennessee Democrats and rural East Tennessee Republicans worked well together. That certainly was true for decades. Tennessee would benefit if it happened more today.

ATTACK OF OBAMA VISIT TYPICAL FOR TODAY'S GOP (2014)

The distinguished Tennessee Republican Party chairman, in a January 29 op-ed in *The Tennessean,* blasted the president of the United States for "campaigning" in coming to a Nashville public school. But the president no longer has to campaign—the American people already re-elected him.

Three-fourths of the GOP chairman's op-ed attacks President Obama and is another example of how a once reasonable and respected Republican Party has become a Tea Party not of ideas but of extreme ideology, not of solutions but of unthinking opposition, not of bipartisan cooperation but of endless antagonism.

Unlike the chairman, the students and faculty at McGavock High School appreciated the President of the United States coming to Tennessee. As the students listened to the president tell of overcoming struggles and trials during childhood—raised by a single mother, his family too often barely scraping by—I could see in young eyes the growing belief that they, too, could overcome their obstacles and achieve their own dreams.

Indeed, I was reminded of words often attributed to St. Francis of Assisi: "Preach the Gospel at all times; if necessary use words."

That the African American son of a broken home who barely knew his father was standing before these students as president shouted the good news of the American Dream. His words of opportunity and responsibility echoed his own life's experience.

In one of only two positive paragraphs, the chairman touted recent test scores to claim credit for the results of reforms put into place by Governor Bill Haslam's Democratic predecessor. Governor Phil Bredesen worked with Democratic and Republican legislators and teamed with Tennessee teachers to earn Tennessee one of the first two Race to the Top grants—*before* Governor Haslam even took office.

The chairman also claimed that Republicans have produced a thriving state economy. But we have watched Republican legislators waste most of their time and our tax money focused on increasing the number of places where we can buy booze and pack pistols. Meanwhile, Republicans haven't produced any jobs bills, and our unemployment rate still far exceeds the national average. Furthermore, according to a recent report from *Moody's Analytics*, Tennessee's job creation in 2014 is projected to rank forty-fourth in the nation and dead last in the entire Southeast.

The chairman says Republicans want an "opportunity-for-all" economy to lift up Tennesseans "regardless of ZIP code" through creating "high-performing schools." But in fact, Republicans are undercutting public schools and attacking public schoolteachers, spending our tax dollars on for-profit "virtual schools" that pay their CEO $5 million of our tax dollars each year and are owned by a convicted felon.

And now Republicans want to give away our tax dollars for vouchers to subsidize sectarian schools and segregation academies. And they are abolishing the inheritance taxes for millionaire and billionaire heirs and heiresses to create an "opportunity-for-the-rich" economy, helping a very few who live in certain wealthy ZIP codes (including many out-of-state heirs and heiresses) at the expense of the working- and the middle-class Tennesseans who pay the bill for these government giveaways.

Tennessee Democrats, by contrast, are working to provide real solutions for jobs and education. Democrats are fighting to raise the minimum wage, seeking tax cuts to grow jobs in small businesses, protecting public school students, fighting for pre-K education for our youngest citizens, and demanding that Republicans let 300,000 working Tennesseans and children get health care instead of sending our Medicaid money to New York and California.

Tennessee Democrats aren't wasting time casting partisan stones at someone from Washington who came to learn from, praise, and inspire Tennessee teachers and students. Instead of doing the bidding of moneyed special interests and the mega-rich, Tennessee Democrats are seeking to serve Tennessee families.

—"Attack of Obama Visit Typical for Today's GOP,"
The Tennessean, 7 February 2014.

15
ON LEGISLATING

Behind the passage or defeat of the legislation discussed in this book was the legislating process itself. Following is an essay reflecting on early experiences serving in the legislature, including a narrative of a week in legislative session. The second essay is advice to citizens on engaging with legislators.

DIARY OF A LEGISLATOR: A FRESHMAN LAWMAKER'S PERSONAL ACCOUNT OF ENCOUNTERING THE POLITICAL PROCESS (1988)

Monday, March 30, 4 a.m.: The alarm goes off, but I'm not ready to get up. Negotiations between lobbyists for the nursing home industry and the "nursing home reform coalition" have been going on for several late-night sessions. The legislation is coming to a head, and I'm concerned. Nancy, my bride of almost three months, and I talk about how I should handle the day.

Nancy reminds me that I'm "awfully independent." And that, she says, "is not always appreciated." She is concerned that I might stop thinking for myself, stop trying to do what I think is right. But, she acknowledges, that means more conflict at times. The nursing home reform negotiations are one of those times.

Last night I angered a senior legislator, a friend whose leadership I've tried to follow. My colleague had not expected me to attend the negotiating session.

When he called and I was there, he let me have it. After he had yelled at me and at another person pushing for reform, I was not sure how much of his anger was real and how much was for effect. I suspect both were involved.

But the question now is, how do I work with him today?

5 a.m.: As I drive to my legislative office, I worry about my home county's election commission. I had to recommend three Democrats to serve on the commission. I tried to balance it geographically, but some Democrats thought there ought to have been a Democrat from their town even though the two Republican commissioners already were from that one town and no commissioners would have represented the eastern or southern parts of the county.

I wish there were a way to make everyone happy.

At the office I try to work on the piles of mail, messages, and memos that have accumulated during the session. There is little way to keep my desk clear—except by throwing much of the paper away. I ought to be doing more of that.

By mid-morning, I've been told that yesterday's Memphis paper contained a column with some approving comments about a West Tennessee Republican and me.

I laugh out loud at this legislator and me being praised together. When he and I first met at the start of this session, we'd both heard so many tales about the other that we were afraid to turn our backs. He'd heard Republicans call me a "Liberal Democrat." I'd heard Democrats call him a "Reactionary Republican." Finding ourselves voting together on several issues, we both shook our heads—and each of us wondered what he was doing wrong.

The nursing home bill negotiations this morning move quickly. By early afternoon we have an agreement. When our unofficial but acknowledged leader asks if I want to be a prime sponsor of the "compromise legislation," I have mixed feelings. I know that others pushing for nursing home reform feel that the negotiated bill is the best legislation proposed by any legislator. I just pray the bill is as good as the reformers hope—and as tough as the industry fears.

5 p.m.: I'm rushing back from teaching The Interaction of Religion and Law to divinity and law students at Vanderbilt University. Class ends just before the legislative session starts at five. It is best not to be a pedestrian on Broadway at that time anyway, but it's especially true with me racing from the classroom to the Capitol.

Talk about switching gears: I'm going from students to lobbyists, from teachers to legislators. Fundamental questions in my class are: "How do you rightly use biblical understandings in creating secular law? What does the Bible say that guides us in drafting legislation on this issue?"

Those questions, quite frankly, are not necessarily the most prominent for me downtown. Instead, two often unspoken but always present questions are, "Will it cost me votes back home?" and "Can an opponent use it against me next election?"

Tonight on the House floor we move fairly quickly through the calendars.

9 p.m.: After the session ends, I go to the three jillionth reception of the session. Some of the sergeants at arms cook hamburgers on the roof of a hotel. Inside, legislators, staffers, lobbyists, and others eat, drink, talk, and watch a basketball game. I visit with a couple of friends from my district, watch the ball game, and talk with a college student intern and others.

Receptions are an interesting phenomenon. It is important for me to know my colleagues—and for them to know me. People need to know me to trust me. And I need to know them to learn whom I can trust and whom I need to watch more carefully. I've already learned one legislator to watch. He slipped in an amendment increasing legislative pensions without disclosing what he was doing. And many of us, particularly the freshmen, did not realize what he'd done until we read about it or until someone told us the next week.

10:30 p.m.: I leave the reception and head home to Nancy.

Tuesday, March 31, 5 a.m.: Fighting with piles of paper on my desk. Still losing.

7 a.m.: The Rural West Tennessee Democratic Caucus meets every Tuesday at this time. The floor is open for the dozen Democratic legislators who represent districts between the Mississippi and Tennessee rivers, excluding Memphis, to share concerns and information.

8 a.m.: Calendar and Rules Committee. A bill I'm sponsoring dealing with abandoned mineral rights is scheduled for consideration. Property titles often are unclear because, long ago, mineral rights were separated from surface rights. Businesses and others sometimes won't buy land, and financial institutions often won't lend money for it, when titles are unclear. Businesses and small folks owning surface rights need help. The coal industry lobbyists are opposing us.

Representative Jerry Jared, a veteran sponsoring the legislation with me, recommends we delay voting on the bill a week. Jerry thinks we don't have the votes to get the bill out of committee. I take his counsel and delay the vote so we can work the committee members a little harder.

10:30 a.m.: Another Southern politician once said that persons holding elected office are largely "fearful" people. Maybe that helps explain my vote today in the Education Committee.

Speaker pro tempore Lois DeBerry has a bill up that would require school boards to adopt some sort of "family life curriculum"—a sex education program.

162   LEADERSHIP

If school systems failed to create their own program, then the state's program would take effect.

The legislation, as amended, would give local school boards the opportunity to deal with this issue however they and the local communities see fit. If they don't like the state's program, they can create their own.

It sounds reasonable enough, especially when there are countless teen pregnancies, hundreds of thousands of abortions each year, and children aren't being instructed or encouraged at home or school or even church to abstain from sex.

But some of the same friends and brothers and sisters in Christ who join me in regretting the countless abortions also lobby against this bill.

When I think the bill has enough votes to pass without my vote, I vote against it. The thought in my mind is, *If my vote isn't necessary, then there's no reason to give an opponent a campaign issue to distort against me next time.*

So, today I vote wrong.

Afterward, I tell DeBerry that I realize I should have voted for the bill. And I reflect on what is happening.

So much is going on. So little time for reflection and considering what is right. Some weeks I may vote on over 200 bills. There can be as many as 150 bills on the consent and regular calendars on the House floor alone, plus the bills in my two committees and in the three subcommittees on which I serve. How do I make time to study enough and talk with resource people enough to make sure the votes I'm casting are faithful and right?

4 p.m.: With Representatives Burnett and Williams and Gordon Bonnyman of the Nursing Home Reform Coalition, I head into the "lion's den" of a nursing home industry board. Its executive director is concerned that the board might not approve what he has negotiated with us—and so are we.

When it is my turn to speak to the board, I probably handle it poorly. I tell them that, if they don't like the bill that has been agreed upon, then they should see what I would like for them to have. I learn later that this feels to them like a threat.

Downstairs in the same hotel, Burnett, Williams, Billy Stair of the Governor's staff, and I discuss what has happened and wait to learn whether the industry will support our bill.

A state employee moonlights as the hotel's piano player, and eventually Representative Williams sings. She has a great voice, and we are all impressed. Then word comes of the industry's decision to support the bill. That means passage is assured. I want to sing, too.

Wednesday, April 1, 8:30 a.m.: On Wednesday mornings the Freshmen Caucus meets to get to know and hear administrators and leaders. No lobbyists. My colleagues were kind enough to elect me chairman.

This morning our speaker is Governor McWherter. I've known him all my life, living down the street from him and his mother in Dresden. Governor McWherter stresses to us new legislators "communication." He says it is crucial, that one has "to work on it every single day."

This Saturday, I'll have a round of open meetings in the district. At those I'll share with people what has been happening in the Legislature, and I'll listen to their concerns. Communication with my colleagues on the hill, however, is more complex. I don't know how to do that so well yet. Actions without relationships can be misunderstood. Miscommunication and the lack of communication can cause problems.

9:15 a.m.: I have to leave the meeting before the Governor finishes. In General Welfare Committee, our nursing home bill is coming up, and I also have a bill up that deals with AIDS.

Early in the session a couple of AIDS bills were introduced, but they didn't seem on target. So I called up the Department of Health and Environment and met with their key people in this area. Then I proposed a bill to require the reporting of AIDS to the state while providing anonymity and confidentiality to the patients.

It was a modest proposal, something already done by forty-nine other states, I was told. But, while a regulation requiring reporting had been proposed in Tennessee, it had not yet been approved.

This morning, though, my bill is "on notice" for the full committee; the special study subcommittee chair wants me to leave my bill in his subcommittee longer. And so I agree.

Also this morning, with lots of press in a packed room, the General Welfare Committee passes our nursing home reform bill.

5 p.m.: After session, I go by the office to return some phone calls, and then I attend a series of receptions. First is a "Slopception" to help get things under way for the "Swine Ball," which will raise thousands of dollars for the American Cancer Society.

After a while, Representative Bill Purcell and I go together to the Black Caucus Reception, where we see colleagues and friends and the Governor. I dance with another legislator, and she seems surprised that this preacher can dance.

9 p.m.: Dinner with the Rural West Tennessee Democratic Caucus and Governor McWherter.

At the end of the author's rookie year and the struggles described in "Diary of a Legislator," the sponsors and supporters of Governor McWherter's nursing-home reform legislation gathered for the bill signing. Those joining Governor McWherter included Commissioner of Health Jim Word, Representative Karen Williams, Senator Joe Haynes, Representative Tommy Burnett, Representative Paul Starnes, and the author. Photo: State of Tennessee Photographic Services.

When I get home about ten, there are phone messages. I return the first call, and it is an hour later before the conversation ends. A couple of good friends are upset over my recommendations on the election commission. Nancy thinks I handled the conversation—and the recommendations—poorly.

Thursday, April 2: After session, I meet with Commissioner Charles Smith and one of his assistants with the Department of Education. They are interested in one of my "caption bills" (bills without much substance but which allow legislators to amend bills in substance after the bill-filing deadline). This bill deals with illiteracy.

Commissioner Smith asks me to wait on my legislation. He says the administration will have legislation prepared for the next session and would like to move then. I am not eager to wait. I doubt anything is more fundamental to our efforts in education or economic development than creating a literate citizenry. But I trust the commissioner. He assures me that they want me to work with them on the legislation and in the effort to attack illiteracy.

That effort needs to be a partnership between government, teachers, and volunteers. I don't want government to stifle private initiative—nor do I want government to be seen as responsible in such a way that private citizens don't get involved.

6 p.m.: I had hoped to attend a Future Farmers banquet or another dinner in West Tennessee, but I simply do not get enough done to feel good about leaving. Finally, I head for my car. Then I see Bill Purcell. His week has been about as crazy as mine, and we decide to eat together.

As we drive to the Gerst Haus, an East Nashville eatery with considerable political history, we discover that both our wives have gone to Jackson—his wife to Jackson, Mississippi, and mine to Jackson, Tennessee. We laugh about yet another strange coincidence.

Bill and I had started together at Vanderbilt Law School. While in law school, we'd both worked at Spencer Youth Center in Nashville giving legal advice to children adjudged delinquent. One evening as we returned from Spencer, we realized that, while each of us thought the other was married, neither was. (I thought he was married because he drove a station wagon; he thought I was married because I was in divinity school.)

We both went with West Tennessee Legal Services after law school, then eventually went into private practices. After we were elected last year, we both married West Tennessee natives named Miller who had known each other while working together in a group home for juveniles in Jackson, Tennessee.

The parallels have not stopped. Now, three months through the session, we both are wrestling our new jobs. We talk about how, for a single legal case, involving just one of our clients, we will spend hours and days preparing. And now at the Capitol, we struggle just to make sure we read the bills and try to ask the right questions before voting on something that may affect over 4.5 million Tennesseans. Misery loves company, and I enjoy Bill's company.

Friday, April 3, 4 a.m.: I get up and drive the almost 150 miles home. Today I work in my Dresden law office, trying to take care of clients who need me and whom I need in order to make a living. The $1,000 a month I get in legislative salary (not counting reimbursement for some expenses) does not begin to pay my office overhead. So early in the mornings, late at nights, on Fridays, and on weekends, I do what I can to keep from using up savings while in session.

As I scramble today, I remember a conversation with a veteran legislator earlier during the session. This legislator had told me: "We talk about a citizen legislature. But there's not any real working men up here. A working man can't afford to be up here."

So, today I try to make a living. Still many folks in the district need to talk with me while I'm home. As a result, I neither get the work done that I'd hoped, nor do I talk with as many friends and constituents as they—or I—would like.

Saturday, April 4, 5 a.m.: Nancy and I are between Dresden and McLemoresville, the site of our first open meeting today. The people of McLemoresville, a community of about five hundred, were gracious to me during the campaign. And this morning when Nancy and I get to City Hall at 5:40 a.m., the mayor and others treat us like family.

After a delicious breakfast served by the volunteer firemen, I stand and speak about recent legislative action to the twenty or so gathered. Then I ask for their questions or comments. I've discovered that in these meetings I often learn more from the people than they learn from me.

7:10 a.m.: Nancy and I drive on to Lavinia, where McLemore's Store and the post office comprise the business district. In my primary election, I got 90 percent of the vote in this precinct against four opponents. Suffice it to say that I have warm feelings for these people.

When I get to McLemore's Store this morning, some of them also have warm feelings for me. *Real* warm. Between thirty and forty people are gathered in the parking lot. I was expecting a crowd but not this many.

I get out of the car and wade into the crowd and shake the hand of everyone there except for one person who declines. I ask how everyone is and smile and love on them like I think they are there to kiss me instead of kick me. Somebody comments that I'm in awfully good spirits, and I tell them I'm glad to see so many friends.

When I begin my remarks, I tell the crowd I'm not sure they have all come just to meet my bride. That brings some laughter. I tell them how long Nancy and I have been married—three months, sixteen hours, thirty-four minutes, and seventeen seconds—and that Nancy says the only folks she knows who keep up with the time that closely are awaiting parole. There is some more laughter.

Finally, hoping some are a little less angry, I ask if anyone is concerned about anything besides the possible school district property tax increase. No one says anything.

The school board has asked me to pass a local bill in the General Assembly to allow it to raise property tax rates by up to a dollar. The school board's concern is that they must be able to hold total revenues steady if the county cuts back its financial support or if the property assessor lowers appraisals on farm property.

The citizens in Lavinia are upset because they'd been told years earlier that increases in the tax rate would have to be approved by referendum. And many are upset because they cannot make ends meet now.

Some are going deeper in debt each year, unable to make loan payments, and some are about to suffer foreclosure and bankruptcy. To them, increasing the property tax rates sounds like another nail in the coffin of debt and expenses.

Others are retired, on fixed incomes, and fear such an increase will hit them hard, too. And it could.

I tell them I am there to listen, and I want to hear their concerns and work with them to try to figure out what we need to do together for the good of everyone. I assure them I'd really like to pass a law that would let the rate be determined by referendum, but the Tennessee Supreme Court had ruled that unconstitutional. And while it would be easiest for me politically and would get me out of the middle to have a referendum, I also have taken an oath to uphold the Constitution. I tell them I cannot and will not pass a law I know to be unconstitutional. Furthermore, I explain, an unconstitutional referendum of no effect would just waste taxpayers' dollars.

The people demand to know what I am going to do. I tell them I'm going to have a meeting in Nashville with the property assessor, members of the school board, the school superintendent, a legislative lawyer, Senator Milton Hamilton, and any and all of them that will come. I ask three of the leaders if they will commit to meet with us, and they agree. I invite everyone else to come, too.

5:19 p.m.: After seven open meetings, Nancy and I are driving back to Nashville so I can speak at a banquet for the Young Democrats State Convention. As I drive back and work on my speech, I think about James MacGregor Burns' book, *Leadership*. Burns distinguishes between "transforming" and "transactional" leadership.

As I reflect on my votes in committee and even on the floor, I worry about being more involved in transactional than transforming leadership. And I worry about whether I've been involved in that today down at the store in Lavinia.

I worry about voting on the basis not of *conscience* but of *campaigning*. Too often I imagine a vote can be attacked with newspaper ads and radio spots. Put another way, I worry about voting on what is the best *politics* instead of what is the best *policy*.

Tonight, at the Young Democrats, I talk about the need for leadership. For people who will lead and will pursue just laws. I preach a sermon meant for the preacher at least as much as for the congregation.

Sunday, April 4: Since I have to be in Nashville again tomorrow, I do not return home to the district today. Instead, I go to early church with a small congregation where I can wear blue jeans. (If the Lord needed the Sabbath, I certainly need one day a week without a suit and necktie.)

By 11 a.m. I'm at the legislative office. I work without lunch and through the afternoon. I felt guilty earlier about not getting up and working several hours before church, like I usually do. That way usually I can take Sunday afternoon for recreation and re-creation.

But this morning I was worn out. Nancy even got up before I did—the first time that has ever happened.

I recall what Governor McWherter, who served our district for eighteen years, often says: It is a *privilege* to serve in the General Assembly. He's right.

Once again, Charlie Daniel understood what public servants experienced and sometimes struggled against. Illustration by Charlie Daniel, *Knoxville News Sentinel*.

In this cartoon, Charlie Daniel captured common public perceptions
and sentiments shared by many legislators, especially late in the session.
Illustration by Charlie Daniel, *Knoxville News Sentinel.*

Discipline. I need more discipline. And I need to figure out how to make
more time to be with my wife.

I look on my calendar at next week. It looks like it will be more demanding
than the one just past.

—"Diary of a Legislator: A Freshman Lawmaker's
Personal Account of Encountering the Political Process,"
Southern Magazine, May 1988.

TIPS ON THE CARE AND FEEDING OF LEGISLATORS (1988)

1. HAVE PATIENCE. Legislators are pulled and tugged, requested and demanded, beseeched and besought. When they don't immediately do exactly
as you would like them to do, be patient with them. Almost all of them are
trying to do good, and the vast majority of them are trying to do right. If they

are trying to do right, then they have more tugs on them than they have coats or shirt-tails to tug. Be patient with them.

2. BE PERSISTENT. The tool that goes with patience is persistence. If you cannot see them when you want to, or if you cannot get your call returned or your letter responded to when you would like, be persistent. Polite, but persistent.

3. BE CLEAR. There are 1,400 or more bills pending at any time. (In the second year of a two-year Assembly, there may be 2,000 bills pending.) When the session gets warmed up, legislators sometimes vote on as many as two hundred or more pieces of legislation in a single week. So try to be as clear as possible about the legislation you want to discuss.

For example, don't just give the bill number and don't just say "the bill that deals with insurance" or something equally vague. It may be the only insurance bill you are looking at, but it may be one of dozens the legislator is trying to consider.

4. BE CONCISE. With all the tugs on a legislator's time almost any legislator will doubly appreciate a constituent or a concerned citizen who is concise. Someone who comes directly to the point, states one's views and ideas with as few words as possible, one who makes clear his or her request.

5. VISIT. The best way to communicate with a legislator and have the greatest impact is to visit. It will show that you care enough to come and see the legislator. Preferably, the visitor will come to the legislative office or when the legislator is having a meeting with constituents or clearly is out for the purpose of dealing with legislation or working as a legislator. Next best would be at the legislator's place of business or work. Probably the last choice is at the legislator's home, unless one is awfully close with that person. Then it doesn't matter if you see the legislator in person or not.

6. CALL. A telephone call is next best, but don't call on Sunday unless you've tried a couple or three times during the week to no avail. And do not call at home unless you've tried at the place of business or legislative office and cannot get a response any other way—legislators need time with their families.

7. WRITE. If you have trouble reaching a legislator, do not hesitate to write. Often, they are awfully busy, and they will appreciate your taking the time to write. Anytime you talk with a legislator in person or by phone, follow up with a letter or email.[1] Make sure you state clearly and concisely your goal, interest, or request.

---

1   This column was written before email, but updated for today's email world.

8. CONTRIBUTE. If you can, contribute financially or by volunteering when your legislators campaign.

There is nothing immoral or wrong about that. It's a way of participating in a democracy.

—"Tips on the Care and Feeding of Legislators,"
Community Economic Reporter, March/April 1988.

CONCLUSION

I appeal to you therefore, brothers and sisters,
by the mercies of God,
to present your bodies as a living sacrifice,
holy and acceptable to God,
which is your spiritual worship.
Do not be conformed to this world,
but be transformed by the renewing of your minds,
so that you may discern what is the will of God—
what is good and acceptable and perfect.

Romans 12:1–2

This country needs far less partisanship and much more patriotism, less enmity and more comity, less yelling at or about the other party and more listening to and learning from the other party.

No party has a monopoly on judgment or truth. We often can learn the most not from supporters but from opponents even during elections and debates. And that is the strength and beauty of America, of democracy, of God's world.

I am a Christian, indeed once was an ordained minister. I do not mean to exclude others, but I do wish to write truthfully from my views and values and experiences as a Christian.

I have heard people ask, "How can someone be a Christian and a *Democrat*?" I have heard others ask, "How can someone be a Christian and a *Republican*?" Frankly, I think it makes more sense to be a Christian and either a Democrat or a Republican than to be a Christian and have no interest in political issues at all.

Is God a Republican? Is God a Democrat? You would think God was one or the other, given how many people claim God is on their side. Furthermore, many are sure God hates the same people they hate. If you find yourself thinking that way, consider the Christian writer Anne Lamott's observation that "You can safely assume you've created God in your own image when it turns out that God hates all the same people you do."[1]

It is safe to say that God is not greatly impressed with either Republicans or Democrats. God is not on the side of any political party but on the side of justice, compassion, truth, mercy, freedom, and life. I am reminded that, when Abraham Lincoln overheard a clergyman say he hoped "the Lord is on our side," President Lincoln responded, "I know that the Lord is always on the side of the right. But it is my constant anxiety and prayer that this nation should be on the Lord's side."

That should also be our prayer.

Christians too often put our hopes in political parties and ideologies. In the 1960s and 1970s, issues of social justice, like civil rights, hungry children, and the Vietnam War, were at the forefront in many churches. Some Christians looked to Democrats and liberal politics to speak the truth of God to society.

In the 1980s and 1990s, issues relating to sexual morality, including abortion, promiscuity, and sexual orientation, were at the forefront in many churches. Some Christians thought Republicans and conservative politics were the keys to redeeming society.

Politics didn't save us in the last century, and it won't save us in this one. But that does not mean people of faith should not be involved in politics. Believers are called into the political arena as in every other area of life. We should not just *be* there, we should be committed and passionate. But our commitment should ultimately be to something much higher than political party or ideology.

I could write an essay on how my many Republican friends can be and are Republicans. Or how, if I'd grown up in East Tennessee or in a different era in West or Middle Tennessee, I could have been Republican.

When I read these collective essays, however, I was surprised how often, particularly in recent years, I called on Republicans, especially "Tea Party Republicans," to step up.

When I was in the legislature, on anything difficult, I sought—and almost always found—Republican colleagues to join me in sponsoring legislation. When

---

1   Anne Lamott, *Bird by Bird: Some Instructions on Writing and Life* (New York: Pantheon Books, 1994).

I was trying to pass a bill, looking for votes, I went to Republican colleagues as quickly and often even more quickly than to fellow Democrats.

But near the end of my legislative tenure, Republican senators met behind closed doors and decided or were told how they would vote on the floor. And then in open sessions, rarely was dissent or independence allowed.

One Republican observer told me he was amused during debates when I would speak and he thought some of my Republican colleagues would realize they were wrong on policy. But, the Republican observed, his fellow Republicans would really squirm when they were locked into voting not just for bad policy but realized it also was going to be bad politics.

There have always been closed-door meetings. But they used to be the exception and not the rule, particularly after then Speaker Ned McWherter led changes to open up meetings and records and government. During my service, until about 2010, it simply was not so partisan so often.

To be sure, Democrats and Republicans from time to time have felt partisan pressures. But now such partisanship seems not the exception but the rule.

Tennessee long has benefited from leaders more concerned about right and wrong than right and left, more concerned about doing right than doing what others tell them to do. We need bipartisan cooperation and bipartisan leadership again. I believe we will be governed that way again. I pray it will be soon.

As we have seen in Washington, long decades of progress can be undone in mere days of cowardice or capitulation. Tennessee does not need to follow Washington's ways. Potomac Fever in Washington ought not be contagious and cause Cumberland Fever in Nashville. We have done better, and we can do better again.

When we recognize that no party or ideology holds all God's truth, then we may even be willing to work together for the good of all God's children.

May it be so.

INDEX

Page numbers in **boldface** refer to illustrations.

Adams, Abigail, 8
Adams, President John, 8
Agricultural Age, 115
American Northerners, 21
American Southerners, 21
Anderson, Dr. Allen, 44
Annis, Professor J. Lee, Jr., 146
Appalachian Spring (Copeland), 33
Aristotle, 26

Baicker, K., 78n2
Ballotpedia, 107n3
Baptists, 9, 31, 96
Better Schools program, 111
biblical figures
    Abraham, 31
    Amos, 137
    Apostle Paul, 91, 151
    Apostles, 155
    eighth-century prophets, 155
    Hebrew prophets, 137
    Hosea, 137
    Israelites, 131
    Jesus, 24, 30, 31, 149, 151, 154, 155
    Micah, 137
    Moses, 74
biblical references
    Deuteronomy 23:19–20, 131
    Deuteronomy 30:19, 74
    Ecclesiastes 1:9, 1n1
    Exodus 22:25–27, 131
    Ezekiel 18:8–17; 22:12, 131

1 Corinthians 13, 32
1 John 3:16, 152
Galatians 3, 91, 151
John 3:16, 149, 152
Matthew 25, 24, 150, 154, 155
Nehemiah 5:6–13, 131
Psalm 23, 32
Romans 12:1–2, 173
biblical references, topical
    Bible, 29, 32, 33, 34, 91, 132, 160
    Christ's Gospel, 150
    Ecclesiastes, 2
    God's truth, 175
    God's Word, 74
    Golden Rule, 74, 149
    Good Book, 31
    Good News, the, 151
    Gospel, 157
    Hebrew Bible, 131
    Hebrew laws, 155
    Jesus's teaching, 155
    Judgment of the Nations, the, 155
    New Testament, 9, 24
    Old Testament law, 137
    Pentateuch, 131
    Sacred Writings, 8, 33
    Scripture, 137, 152
    Scriptures, the, 151
    Sermon on the Mount, 32
    See also Christian figures in art
        and music; God
Binkley, Josephine, 56
Bonnyman, Esquire, Gordon, 162
Bredesen administration, 135
Buchanan, Patrick, 25

Burns, James MacGregor, 167
Butler, President Walter, 62

Caldwell, Leigh Ann, 88n3
Career Ladder, 111
Catholics, 19
caucuses
    Black Caucus, 163
    Freshman Caucus, 163
    Rural West Tennessee
        Democratic Caucus, 157,
        161, 163
Charlier, Tom, 126
Chicago Bulls, 31
Christian, 17, 19, 20, 151, 152, 154, 173, 174
Christian figures in art and music
    Davinci's *Madonna of the Rocks*,
        33
    Handel's *Messiah*, 33
    Michelangelo's Sistine Chapel, 33
    Milton's *Paradise Lost*, 32
    Rembrandt's *Return of the
        Prodigal Son*, 33
    See also biblical references,
        topical; God
Churchill, Sir Winston, 4
Citibank, 132
cities
    Appomattox, VA, 24
    Belfast, Ireland, 17
    Charlottesville, VA, 23
    Chicago, IL, 132, 133
    Cleveland, OH, 84, 119
    Dresden, East Germany, 19
    East Berlin, East Germany, 20
    Flint, MI, 52
    Milwaukee, WI, 119
    New Orleans, LA, 23, 119
    Seattle, WA, 20
    Waldenburg, AR, 84
    Washington, DC, 7
    See also cities (TN)

cities (TN)
    Bristol, TN, 169
    Chattanooga, TN, 50, 134
    Clarksville, TN, 50
    Dresden, TN, 3, 19, 127, 142, 143,
        163, 165, 166
    Greenfield, TN, 101, 128
    Huntingdon, TN, 62
    Jackson, TN, 49, 165
    Lavinia, TN, 166, 167
    McKenzie, TN, 61, 63
    McLemoresville, TN, 62, 166
    Memphis, TN, 23, 50, 87, 91, 105,
        134
    Nashville, TN, 7, 50, 87, 90, 157,
        165, 167, 168, 169
    Palmersville, TN, 143
    Somerville, TN, 49
    See also cities
Civil War, 21, 23, 24
class warfare, 155
Cobler, Nicole, 88n1
Commercial Appeal. See under media
communists, 19, 20
Confederate Park, 24
Confederate statues, 23
Constitution of the State of Tennessee,
    93, 99, 101, 102, 104, 107, 167
    Article One at Section 35, 107
Constitution of the United States, 15,
    27, 30, 33, 89, 132, 152, 156
    Bill of Rights, 103
    Establishment Clause, 30, 31, 33
    First Amendment, 17, 30
    Fourteenth Amendment, 103
    Free Exercise Clause, 30, 33, 98
    Nineteenth Amendment, 103
    Second Amendment, 98
    Sixth Amendment, 27
    Thirteenth Amendment, 103
Corporation for Enterprise
    Development, 142

Costco, 124
counties (TN)
    Carroll County, TN, 3, 61, 62
    Decatur County, TN, 84
    Fayette County, TN, 49
    Hamilton County, TN, 85
    Henry County, TN, 61
    Pickett County, TN, 85
    Shelby County, TN, 49
    Weakley County, TN, 3, 61, 90,
      105, 125
countries and states
    China, 127
    Czech Republic, 18
    Czechoslovakia, 16, 18, 19, 20
    East Germany, 15, 20, 21
    Ireland, 18
    Israel, 131
    Japan, 15, 21, 23, 113, 114, 115
    Mexico, 52
    Philippines, 18, 19
    Poland, 15, 20
    Russia, 16, 21
    Scotland, 9, 24
    Slovak Republic, 15, 18
    Soviet Union, 16, 21
    See also regions; states (US)
court cases
    Planned Parenthood of Middle
      Tennessee, et al. v. Don
      Sundquist, Governor of the
      State of Tennessee, et al., 93
    Roe v. Wade, 98, 99
Crockett, Davy, 126
Cumberland Fever, 175
Czechs, 15

Daniel, Charlie, **34, 43, 46, 48, 57, 58,**
  70, 79, 80, 86, 89, 92, 100, 115, 116,
  129, 168, 169
Decker, Dr. Michael, 44
Declaration of Independence, 8

Donahue, Reverend Professor John, 26
Dow Jones, 142
Dubcek government, 16

Earned Income Tax Credit, 124
Easley, Rebecca, 105
Emancipation Proclamation, 156
Epstein, A. M., 78n2

family, author's
    Brasfield, "Miss" Johnnie, 4
    Herron, Ben Miller, 112
    Herron, Chancellor Grooms, 4,
      9, 53, 54, 55, 73
    Herron, Dean, 153
    Herron, Esquire, Clarence B., 4
    Herron, John Miller, 3, 112, 113
    Herron, Mary Brasfield, 4, 54,
      73, 85, 86, 87, 113
    Herron, Rick Miller, 112, 113, 117
    Hickman, Betsye Herron, 54, 55, 153
    Miller-Herron, Nancy Carol, 9,
      94, 97, 150, 153, 159, 165, 166,
      167, 169
Fant, Dean Gene, 32
Forrest, General Nathan Bedford, 24
Fort Donelson, 22
founders, 8, 15
Franklin, Benjamin, 8, 33

Gallup, George, 32
Gap, 124
Gardella, Rich, 88n3
Gerst Haus, 165
God, 128, 129, 156, 174
    Almighty God, 91, 94
    Creator, 129
    God's children, 155, 175
    God's World, 173
    See also biblical references,
      topical; Christian figures in
      art and music

Good Friday Agreement, 18, 19
Goodspeed's 1887 *History of Tennessee*, 126
Gore, Karenna, 6
Gore, Kristen, 6
Gore, Sarah, 6
Gore, Tipper, 6
government agencies and institutions, federal
    Centers for Medicare and Medicaid Services, 61
    Congressional Budget Office, 59
    Constitutional Convention, 8, 33
    Legal Services Corporation, 24, 26
    National Highway Traffic Safety Administration, 44, 47
    National Traffic Safety Administration, 42
    National Transportation Safety Board, 49
    Social Security Administration, 25
    United States Supreme Court, 26, 89, 98
    US House of Representatives, 60
    US Senate, 60
government agencies and institutions, state
    Bureau of Tenncare, 68
    House Calendar and Rules Committee, 161
    House Education Committee, 161
    House General Welfare Committee, 163
    House Judiciary Committee, 101
    Joint Predatory Lending Study Committee, 134
    North Carolina Board of Elections, 88
    State Board of Education, 33
    State of Tennessee Photographic Services, 56, 164

    Tennessee Commissioner of Transportation, 50
    Tennessee Department of Education, 164
    Tennessee Department of Health, 87
    Tennessee Department of Health and Environment, 44, 163
    Tennessee Department of Health Office of Vital Records, 87
    Tennessee Department of Safety, 50, 86, 87
    Tennessee Department of Transportation, 49
    Tennessee Senate Health and Human Services Committee, 63
    Tennessee Supreme Court, 167
Gray, Anita, 136
Great Depression, 4, 153
Great Recession, 154
Great Seal of the United States, the, 91
Groseclose, Deborah, 105

Haltom, Bill, 147
Harvard School of Public Health, 74
Havel, Vaclav, 18
Hensley, Tom "The Golden Goose," 40
hospitals
    Copper Basin Medical Center, Copperhill, TN, 77
    Cumberland River Hospital, Celina, TN, 77
    Decatur County General Hospital, Decaturville TN, 77
    Donelson General Hospital, Nashville, TN, 45
    Erlanger Hospital, Chattanooga, TN, 45, 56
    Gibson General Hospital, Trenton, TN, 76
    Haywood Park Community Hospital, Brownsville, TN, 76

Humboldt General Hospital,
Humboldt, TN, 76
Jamestown Regional Medical
Center, Jamestown, TN, 77
McKenzie Regional Hospital,
McKenzie, TN, 62, 77
Parkridge West Hospital, Jasper,
TN, 77
Starr Regional Medical Center,
Etowah, TN, 76
Takoma Regional Hospital,
Greeneville, TN, 77
Tennova Healthcare-McNairy
Regional Hospital, Selmer,
TN, 77
United Regional Medical Center,
Manchester, TN, 77
University of Tennessee Medical
Center, 44
Vanderbilt University Medical
Center, 44, 45, 47, 76, 78
How Can a Christian Be in Politics?, 8n2

Industrial Age, 115
Information Age, 115
inheritance taxes, 158
interest groups
American Association of Retired
Persons (AARP), 106
American Bar Association
(ABA), 26
American Cancer Society, 58, 163
American Civil Liberties Union
(ACLU), 31, 103
American Heart Association, 58
American Legion, 22
American Lung Association, 58
Big Tobacco, 54
BlueCross BlueShield, 69
Christian Coalition, 31
Future Farmers of America
(FFA), 165

Insurance Institute for Highway
Safety, 48n3
Mothers Against Drunk Driving
(MADD), 106
National Victims' Center, 106
Nursing Home Reform Coalition,
162
Tennessee Association of Chiefs
of Police, 106
Tennessee Chamber of
Commerce, 55
Tennessee District Attorneys
General Conference, 106
Tennessee Hospital Alliance, 80
Tennessee Hospital Association
(THA), 56, 80
Tennessee Medical Association
(TMA), 56
Tennessee Restaurant
Association, 55, 58
Tennessee Sheriffs' Association,
106
IRA, 17
Iron Curtain, 15, 16, 19, 21

Jennings, Garrett, 125
Jewish Community Centers, 31
Jews, 31
Jordan, Michael, 31
Judd, Alan, 88n2

Kilpatrick, James, 26
Kimelman, Jeremia, 88n3
King, Rev. Dr. Martin Luther, Jr., 90
Knoxville News Sentinel. See under
media
Koizumi, Prime Minister Junichiro, 22
Kyo, 113

Lamott, Anne, 174
LaVelle, Dr. David, 49
LaVelle, Jenny, 49

LaVelle, Liz, 49
leadership, 167
Legal Services, 25, 27
legislation, federal
    Affordable Care Act, 53, 58, 59,
        60, 61, 78
    Civil Rights Act of 1964, 90, 91,
        92
    GI Bill, 149, 153
    Medicaid, 2, 25, 56, 65, 66, 71,
        72, 73, 74, 75, 78, 79, 80, 124,
        143, 158
    Medicare, 62, 63, 66, 72, 153
    NAFTA, 127
    Obamacare, 6, 58, 80
    Race to the Top, 158
    Social Security, 91, 153
    Voting Rights Act of 1965, 92
legislation, state
    1995 Tennessee Public Acts,
        Chapter 112, 45n2
    2003 Tennessee Public Acts,
        Chapter 299, 45n2
    2007 Tennessee Public Acts,
        Public Chapter 368, 55
    2011 Tennessee Public Acts,
        Chapter 301, 85
    Amendment One, 93, 94, 95, 96,
        97, 98, 99, 100 (*see also* Senate
        Joint Resolution 127)
    Bible in Schools Act, 29, 33, 34
    Cover Tennessee, 56
    Crime Victims' Bill of Rights,
        101, 103, 104, 105, 107 (*see also*
        House Joint Resolution 14)
    Education Savings Accounts
        (ESAs), 116, 117, 118, 119
    House Joint Resolution 14, 102,
        104 (*see also* Crime Victims'
        Bill of Rights)
    Insure Tennessee, 80
    Master Teachers program, 111

Schools First, 54
Senate Joint Resolution 127, 93
    (*see also* Amendment One)
Senate Joint Resolution 2, 104
Student Religious Liberty Act,
    32, 35
Tennessee Children's Product
    Safety Act, 39
Tennessee Code Annotated
    55–10–401, 43n1
Tennessee Non-Smoker
    Protection Act, 53
Tennessee Promise, 113
Tennessee Student Religious
    Liberty Act, 29, 31
Tennessee Voter Confidence Act,
    83, 84, 85, 86
Lombardi, Dr. Sal, 150, 154

Maloan, Richard, 133
McDonald, Ronald, 7
McDonald's, 124
McGavock High School, 157
McLemore's Store, 166
media
    Allison, Natalie, 130n1
    Associated Press (AP), 6
    Atlanta Journal-Constitution,
        88n2
    Chattanooga Times, 10 (*see also*
        Plante, Bruce)
    Chattanooga Times Free Press,
        79, 91, 98
    Christian Lawyer, The, 151, 156
    City and State magazine, 144
    Commercial Appeal, 18, 32,
        50, 62, 68, 74, 85, 88, 91,
        96, 106, 115, 119, 126, 129,
        133, 136, 145
    Community Economic Reporter,
        171
    Governing magazine, 145

Harris, Lena (Associated Press), 6
Jackson Sun, 35, 42, 103
Japan Times, 23
Knoxville News Sentinel, 73, 88, 151 (*see also* Daniel, Charlie)
Liptak, Adam, 89n4, 92n5
NBC News, 88n3
New York Times, 51, 84, 89n4, 92n5
Newsweek Magazine, 60n1
Orlando Sentinel, 116
Royko, Mike, 132, 133
Southern Magazine, 169
Tennessee Bar Journal, 146
Tennessean, The, 27, 45, 47, 52, 55, 57, 60, 76, 99, 115, 117, 125, 130, 137, 151, 157, 158
Texas Tribune, 88n1
Time magazine, 32, 34
TNReport, 91
United Methodist Communications, 21
USA Today, 79
Wall Street Journal, 20, 69
Washington Post, 60n2
Medlin, Carey Ann, 101
Mercedes Benz, 116
Merrick, Dr. Bryan, 61, 62, 63
Methodist Church, 9
Mid-South Fair, 90
Miller, Debbie, 165
minimum wage, 158
Mitchell, Joni, 15
Moody's Analytics, 158
Morris, Dr. John, 47

National Center for Public Policy and Higher Education, 114
National Football League, 114
New Deal, 153
New England Journal of Medicine, 74, 78n2

New York's Hell's Kitchen, 9
95 county jobs program, 129

Oakley, Hannah, 125
Obama administration, 61
officials, federal
    Alexander, Senator Lamar, 39, 40, 42, 62, 111, 125, 141, 157
    Baker, Senator Howard, 5, 24, 114, 141, 142, 145, 146, 156
    Black, Senator Diane, 56, 93n1
    Burchett, Congressman Tim, 58
    Bush, President George W., 125, 154
    Bush, Vice President/President George H. W., 6
    Cheney, Vice President Dick, 154
    Clinton, President Bill, 150, 154
    Corker, Senator Bob, 62, 125
    Eisenhower, President Dwight, 156
    Frist, Senator Bill, 141
    Gore, Senator/Vice President Al, Jr., 6, 18, 133, 140, 141, 150, 154
    Gore, Sr., Senator Albert, 90, 141
    Holmes, Oliver Wendell, 26
    Jefferson, President Thomas, 8, 151
    Johnson, President Lyndon Baines, 19, 90
    Kefauver, Senator Estes, 141
    Kustoff, Congressman David, 62
    Lincoln, President Abraham, 33, 152, 156, 174
    Marcos, President Ferdinand, 18, 19
    McCain, Senator John, 60, 61, 84
    Nixon, President Richard, 26
    Obama, Senator/President Barack, 84, 90, 157, 158
    Powell, Justice Lewis, 26
    Quillen, Congressman Jimmy, 157
    Reagan, President Ronald, 5, 19, 133, 154

officials, federal (*continued*)
  Romney, Governor/Senator Mitt, 58, 60
  Roosevelt, President Franklin, 153
  Roosevelt, President Theodore, 156
  Sasser, Senator Jim, 24, 141
  Tanner, Congressman John, 127, 128
  Thompson, Senator Fred, 141
  Trump, President Donald, 61, 126, 127
  Washington, President George, 8
officials, local
  Biggs, Mayor Mike, 128
  Holland, Mayor Jill, 61n3, 63
  Kelley, Mayor Dale, 62
  McBride, Mayor Kenny, 62
  Williams, Mayor Phil, 62
officials, state
  Alexander, Governor Lamar, 39, 40, 42, 62, 111, 125, 141, 157
  Beavers, Senator Mae, 93n1
  Bredesen, Governor Phil, 54, 56, 58, 111, 119, 158
  Burchett, Senator Tim, 58
  Burks, Representative/Senator Tommy, 95, 104, 106
  Burks, Senator Charlotte, 95, 96, 106
  Burnett, Representative Tommy, 162, 164
  Clement, Governor Frank, 141
  Deberry, Speaker Pro Tem Lois, 161, 162
  Donelson, Commissioner Lewie, 7
  Duncan, Reverend/Representative Ralph, 95
  Faulk, Senator Mike, 42
  Fitzhugh, Representative Craig, 29, 32, 35, 56, 57, 58, 137
  Gibson, Judge Brandon, 130
  Gordon, Director Darren, 70

Hamilton, Senator/Commissioner Milton, 11, 167
Hargett, Secretary of State Tre, 85
Hargrove, Representative Jere, 106
Harwell, Speaker Beth, 75, 76
Haslam, Governor Bill, 5, 6, 51, 77, 80, 113, 118, 119, 123, 125, 158
Haynes, Senator Joe, 164
Hood, Representative John, 56
Ivy, Representative/Commissioner L.H. "Cotton," 12, 30
Jared, Representative Jerry, 161
Jones, Representative Sherry, 51
Lee, Governor Bill, 113, 118, 119, 130
Long, Dr./Director Wendy, 70
Maddox, Representative Mark, 29, 34, 35
McNally, Senator/Lieutenant Governor Randy, 58
McWherter, Governor Ned, 3, 4, 5, 65, 111, 127, 128, 129, 140, 141, 142, 143, 145, 156, 157, 163, 164, 168, 175
Miller, Senator Jeff, 58
Norris, Senator Mark, 56
O'Brien, Senator Anna Belle Clement, 10
Pence, Governor Mike, 5
Purcell, Representative Bill, 163, 165
Ramsey, Lieutenant Governor Ron, 11, 75
Roberts, Director Gabe, 70
Smith, Commissioner Charles, 164
Stair, Senior Policy Advisor Billy, 162
Starnes, Representative Paul, 164
Sundquist, Governor Don, 10, 11, 65, 69, 111
Swann, Representative/Senator Art, 7

Tate, Senator Reggie, 90
Tighe, Deputy Commissioner
    John, 67, 68
Tracy, Senator Jim, 58
Walley, Representative/Senator
    Page, 68
Williams, Representative Karen,
    162, 164
Word, Commissioner Jim, 164
Other Fellow May Be Right, The, 147

Pacific War, 22, 23
Panama Canal, 146
Panera Bread, 124
Paul, II, Pope John, 19
Pilcher, Atha, 49
Pilcher, Jim, 49
Pilcher, Mary Margaret, 49
Plante, Bruce, **10, 11, 35**
Politics (Aristotle), 26
Potomac Fever, 175
pre-K education, 158
Prescott, Esquire, Annie, 87
Protestants, 17, 19
Public Religion Research Institute, 99n3
public schools, 158
Putin, Vladimir, 21

Rand, Ayn, 150, 152
Rayburn, Randy, 58
Reagan administration, 24
Reconstruction, 90
Regional Medical Center, 56
regions
    American South, 23
    East Tennessee, 174
    Eastern Europe, 15, 16, 19, 20,
        21, 68
    Europe, 19
    Far East, 52
    Middle Tennessee, 143, 174
    Northern Ireland, 17, 18, 19

    South, 9, 23, 24
    West Tennessee, 105, 134, 143, 174
    See also countries and states;
        states (US)
Richardson, Debi, 105
Richardson, Roger, 105
Riotta, Chris, 60n1
Rodriguez, Esquire, Rachel, 50
Rogers, Will, 155
Roman Catholics, 9, 17
Rotary International, 24
rural East Tennessee Republicans, 157
Rural Opportunity Summit, 130
rural Tennesseans, 128

Second Continental Congress, 8
Senator Burks's Family, 105
Shakespeare's *Macbeth*, 32
Shelby County Republican Party, 51
Shiloh, 22
Sommers, B. D., 78n2
Southeastern Conference, 114
Southern Democrat, 155
Southern Regional Education Board
    (SREB), 114
Southerner, 22, 23
Spencer Youth Center, 165
St. Francis of Assisi, 157
states (US)
    Alabama, 85
    Alaska, 116
    Arizona, 116, 117
    Arkansas, 55, 84, 114
    California, 55, 85, 158
    Florida, 55, 84, 116, 117
    Georgia, 55, 88
    Idaho, 55, 85
    Illinois, 55
    Indiana, 117
    Iowa, 84
    Louisiana, 117, 119
    Maine, 55

states (US) (*continued*)
    Maryland, 89
    Massachusetts, 58
    Missouri, 50, 85
    Montana, 55
    Nevada, 55
    New Jersey, 84
    New Mexico, 55
    New York, 78, 85
    North Carolina, 85, 88, 89
    North Dakota, 85
    Ohio, 55, 117, 119
    South Carolina, 50
    South Dakota, 55, 85
    Texas, 84, 88
    Utah, 55
    Washington State, 55
    West Virginia, 85
    Wisconsin, 117, 119
    See also countries and states;
      regions
Stevenson, Peter W., 60n2
Stout, Charlotte, 101, 102, 103, 105
Stride Rite, 124
Subway, 124
Sundquist administration, 67
Swafford, Esquire, Claude, 147
Swafford, Esquire, Howard, 147
Swine Ball, 163

Tea Party Republicans, 95, 98, 124, 156, 157, 174
TennCare, 2, 56, 63, 65, 66, 67, 68, 69, 70, 72
TennCare Oversight Committee, 63, 69
TennCare Partners, 67
Tennessee Democratic Party, 151
Tennessee Political Humor, 12
Tennessee Reconnect, 113
Tennessee Republican Party Chairman, 157
Tennessee Titans, 114

Tennessee Treasures, 142
Tennessee Young Democrats, 167, 168
Tennessean, The. See under media
title pledge lending, 136
Trump administration, 61, 80
Twenty-First Century Schools, 111, 142
Tyndale House, 8n2

universities
    Bethel University, 62
    Lipscomb University, 49
    Stanford University, 117
    University of Memphis, 75, 78, 91
    University of Southern California, 91
    University of Tennessee, 147
    University of Tennessee at Knoxville, 24
    University of Tennessee at Martin, 24, 127
    University of Tennessee Volunteers, 114

Vanderbilt Univeristy
    Interaction of Religion and Law class, the, 160
    Vanderbilt Law and Divinity program, 150
    Vanderbilt Law School, 165
    Vanderbilt University, 24, 99, 114, 160
Vietnam War, 174
virtual schools, 158
Visa, 132, 133
vouchers, 113, 118, 119, 158

Watergate, 146
West Tennessee Legal Services, 24, 165

Xantus, 67

Yasukuni Shrine, 22

ABOUT THE AUTHOR

Roy Herron studied New Testament and ethics as a Rotary scholar in Scotland, then was one of Vanderbilt University's first two students who graduated from both the law school and the divinity school. Roy has served as a minister and made his living as an attorney.

While in the Tennessee House of Representatives and Tennessee Senate, Roy held over a thousand listening meetings. In twenty-six years, he attended 1,292 floor sessions, missing only the day when his youngest son was being born. His colleagues chose him as their Caucus Chair and their Floor Leader.

The Boston marathoner has finished more than forty marathons and ultra-marathons, as well as ten 140-mile Ironman triathlons. Roy and his wife, Nancy, also a law-divinity graduate who has worked in the ministry and law, have three sons.

Roy's other books are *Things Held Dear: Soul Stories for My Sons, Tennessee Political Humor: Some of These Jokes You Voted For* (with L. H. "Cotton" Ivy), and *God and Politics: How Can a Christian Be in Politics?*